I0413575

Just Like Therapy

Your DIY Guide To A Happier You

Avanti Desai

PARTRIDGE

To order additional copies of this book, contact
Partridge India
000 800 050 4691 (Call Free)
+91 000 80091 90634 (Outside India)
orders.india@partridgepublishing.com

www.partridgepublishing.com/india

This book is designed to be a valuable resource for those seeking to understand and improve their mental well-being. It offers a wealth of information, practical strategies, and exercises to enhance your emotional awareness and resilience. However, it's crucial to recognize that this book is not intended as a diagnostic tool or a substitute for professional therapy. While it can provide valuable insights and support, it cannot replace the expertise of a qualified mental health professional.

Think of this book as a roadmap to navigate your inner landscape. It can equip you with the knowledge and tools to identify emotional patterns, develop healthy coping mechanisms, and cultivate a sense of well-being. Yet, if you encounter complex challenges or suspect a specific mental health condition, seeking professional guidance remains paramount.

Within these pages, you'll discover a comprehensive exploration of mental health, encompassing various topics and techniques. However, the ultimate goal is to empower you to take charge of your mental well-being and, when necessary, seek additional support from qualified professionals. This book serves as a starting point, not the final destination, on your journey towards optimal mental health.

To the heart that aches in the quiet, to the soul bruised by battles unseen, this book is your solace. It's for the tears you've swallowed, the dreams you've held captive, and the strength you never knew you possessed. We've all walked this path, a labyrinth of doubt and fear. Here, you'll find a hand to hold, a voice to remind you – you are worthy, you are enough. Let these pages be a map leading you back to yourself, a gentle whisper urging you to reclaim the light that burns brightly within. You are not broken, you are becoming.

This journey of self-discovery starts now.

Introduction

Feeling tangled in the jungle of jitters? Does life keep throwing pebbles at your peace of mind, turning your days into a stormy sea? We all know the stress monster – that grumpy beast that steals our sunshine and whispers worries in our ears.

Just Like Therapy is your own personal guide, much like an insightful therapist by your side, here to help you untangle the web of stress and find a hidden path to peace. Think of this place as a friendly campfire, a place to explore the whispers of your heart. With exercises and questions that make you think, you'll be like a brave explorer, venturing into the hidden corners of the mind. We'll face the shadows together – those grumpy thoughts that make the stress monster even bigger. But don't worry, this journey won't leave you feeling lost. You'll learn to build a bridge over those grumpy thoughts, plant seeds of happy feelings, and finally quiet the inner voice that keeps saying, "You can't do it!"

Everyone's path is different. Maybe you're just feeling a little stressed, like a cloud is hanging over your head. Or maybe there are bigger worries, like a tangled knot of fear in your tummy. This book has tools for everyone, a backpack full of tricks to manage all kinds of jitters, from the everyday worries that bug you to the butterflies that flutter wildly during a big speech. It's time to take the reins back from the stress monster and be the captain of your own happy ship. This book isn't a magic potion, but it's a warm sunbeam on a cloudy day, a friend who helps you find your way back to the sunshine in your heart. Let's embark on this journey together, exploring the depths of the human mind and paving the road to mental wellness. So, take a deep breath, turn the page, and let's explore the jungle together. You've got this, adventurer!

1

The trigger trap

Escape the cycle of emotional reactivity

Have you noticed how certain topics, especially questions about personal issues, can bring up a variety of unpleasant emotions? These could be conversations about money, jobs, or romantic relationships. For some, it could be hearing about engagements, and so on. These topics can bother us and make us feel angry, jealous, guilty, or sad. Often, these feelings create a strong sense of shame because we think we are not living up to our own expectations or those of others. For example, it is understandable to feel angry when a coworker gets a promotion that you also wanted. We may feel envious and disappointed when we see our best friend get married, especially if we are struggling to find a partner. Whatever triggers these negative feelings in us, we need to ask ourselves, *"What about this person's experiences or blessings makes me so angry?"* By asking this question, we take the first step towards learning to spot our emotional triggers.

What is an emotional trigger?

We all know the feeling. A friend or family member makes a joke or comment that sets us off. We overreact, feel anxious, and become emotionally destabilized for the rest of the day. We all have experiences that can push our buttons.

A *trigger* is anything that makes us feel uncomfortable. It could be an object, a topic, a word, or even a smell that evokes strong negative feelings because it sets off an emotionally upsetting memory of the past. At its heart, triggers are a reaction to past trauma. These triggers hint at the aspects of our life that we feel unsatisfied and frustrated about. When someone triggers us, it is often because they reflect something we have not yet healed within ourselves. The people who trigger us are not doing it to hurt us. They are simply reflecting back to us what we need to heal. They are not our enemies. They are our teachers, and we can use these relationships as an opportunity for growth.

A vast range of experiences can act as triggers, each affecting individuals differently. Not everyone will suddenly feel emotionally stressed because of something they saw on the news, in the media, or in real life. But, when they say they are *triggered*, they usually mean that something suddenly brought on symptoms related to their mental health, such as worsened mood, anxiety, etc.

We all have hot buttons – words or behaviors that spill out a reaction and cause us to either lash out in anger or completely shut down. While we all have emotional triggers, it can be challenging to identify them. Knowing and understanding them can help us heal and respond more healthily. It is also important to understand that triggering isn't always about what is said or done. The story we tell ourselves about what has occurred is what has the most power to shape our lives. When we can identify what bothers us, we can take action to protect our mental health. Our experiences don't have to define us.

Why do we get triggered?

The answer lies in our formative years. As we grew up, we all experienced pain and suffering while learning to navigate new life events. Because we couldn't recognize or handle difficult circumstances at the time, as adults, we often become triggered by situations that bring back those terrible memories. We often turn to unhealthy or addictive behaviors out of habit to cope with this suffering.

Consider these scenarios:

Scenario 1

Jane was raised by unavailable parents. Her mother was emotionally distant, and her father traveled frequently. The lack of affection, tenderness, and warmth in her connection with her parents was evident. Even as a young child, she was often left alone. When her brother was born two years later, she cared for him. She began cooking meals at the age of five, not only for herself but also for her younger sister and brother. She essentially did everything herself.

She is a competent doctor today, but she becomes painfully triggered when a loved one is unavailable. When her college-aged daughter doesn't return her calls, she becomes distraught and angry while blaming her husband for causing the suffering. However, her husband is not to blame.

In this scenario, Jane didn't realize that *unavailability* was her emotional trigger and that she most often tried to avoid her old pain of being ignored by blaming her husband. To heal, she must learn to tenderly care for her inner child.

Scenario 2

Imagine that Michelle redecorated the living room and thoroughly cleaned her flat. She eagerly awaits her partner's reaction when they arrive home from work. Instead, they go to the kitchen for a bite before settling silently onto the sofa. When her efforts go unnoticed, she feels hurt and rejected. She may start to think that her partner doesn't appreciate her efforts or that they don't love her anymore. These thoughts may trigger feelings of anger, sadness, or anxiety.

In this scenario, Michelle's trigger is feeling *unappreciated*. She may have learned this response in her childhood, when her parents didn't always acknowledge her efforts. To heal, she needs to learn to appreciate herself and her own worth.

Scenario 3:

John used to be triggered by anyone's *hostility* or *disapproval*. His parents were both very judgmental, and his mother was especially hot-headed. He would do anything to avoid feeling the loneliness and sadness of someone else's unloving behavior when they were upset with him or disapproved of him. As a child, John often felt helpless and alone. So, when he experienced any level of those emotions as an adult, it would trigger him. He eventually healed himself by learning how to be incredibly loving to his fearful inner child.

Our memories, experiences, and thoughts can all be triggers. We associate the current situation with a past experience that has a similar emotional trigger. For example, let's say you have a strong aversion to public speaking. This fear might stem from a negative experience you had in school during a presentation. If you don't understand the root of this fear, you might simply avoid public speaking situations altogether. However, by understanding the cause, you can begin to address it and potentially overcome your fear. If we don't understand why we react the way we do, we are more likely to blame the situation or the person.

Uncovering your emotional triggers

Identifying your triggers can be challenging, but you can take steps to make it easier. Remember that although you might have just one trigger, it is common for people to have several. Regardless of the trigger's cause or type, recognizing it is the first step in seeking assistance.

From the list below, think about which behaviors are most likely to bring about an emotional reaction in you. Take a moment to reflect on the following: what kind of behaviors make your anger flare, anxiety spike, or your sadness well up?

Being rejected or abandoned	Being ignored	Being criticized	Being blamed	Being yelled at
Silent treatment	Being lied to	Being controlled	Being approached sexually	Being disapproved of
Sarcasm	Being treated unfairly	Being challenged	Being shamed	Being threatened
Being ghosted	Being excluded	Being manipulated	Losing control	Being disrespected

Once you have identified your triggers, pay attention to the feelings they bring up for you. What do you think is your typical response?

- Anger – When you feel you are being mistreated, insulted, played or used
- Pity or sadness – When you consider someone to be weak or defeated
- Shame or guilt – When you feel that you are to be blamed for their emotion
- Defensiveness or hostility – When you believe they are accusing you
- Frustration – When you feel pressured to manage other people's emotions
- Fear – When you anticipate things getting worse
- Any other emotion

Now it's time to reflect on the past memories connected to that trigger. As you go back in time, you will most likely find that your response results from an earlier idea or memory. For example, someone abused as a child may have difficulty trusting people. They may be triggered by raised voices or physical contact, that remind them of the abuse. This can lead to fear, anxiety, or even flashbacks. In this case, the triggering behavior is the *raised voices* or *physical contact*. The past memory is the abuse that the person experienced as a child.

Knowing your triggers will help you protect your mental well-being. This may be an important part of your self-care routine that you have been neglecting. But be patient with yourself. It is not always easy to identify specific triggers, especially when you are feeling overwhelmed by emotions. One way to identify them is to think back to the first time you felt these emotions. Was there a particular moment in your childhood that brought about these feelings? Or was it a more recent occurrence, such as a heated argument with a friend or family member?

Another way to identify your triggers is to pay attention to how you feel in the moment. What are your physical symptoms when you are feeling overwhelmed by emotions? Do you notice a racing heartbeat, shallow breathing, or muscle tension? By examining your physical and cognitive responses, you can start to pinpoint the triggers that are causing you distress. Emotional triggers can also have physical effects on the body. Take some time to review the table below and check any symptoms that you may have experienced in any situation. These physical effects can be a red flag that something is not right.

Pounding heart	Upset stomach	Feeling dizzy	Feeling sick
Trembling or shaking	Sweating	Muscle tension	Cold sweats
Nausea	Headache	Hot flushes	Chest pain
Tingling	Numbness	Chills	Sensations of heat

Why do we react the way we do?

When you are feeling triggered, you may be reliving a traumatic event. Although everyone has individual triggers, many people share similar trigger reactions. Here are some of the most common:

- Feeling fearful, uneasy, and nervous
- Racing heartbeat, sweating, and difficulty breathing
- Feeling like you are losing control over your feelings
- Urge to flee, escape or avoid the trigger or the situation
- Negative automatic thoughts or unexpected changes in mood
- Anxiety or panic attacks
- Muscle tension, such as jaw or fist clenching
- Memories and flashbacks of upsetting or painful experiences
- Delayed anger outbursts or sadness

Triggering events can cause a variety of reactions, including depression, irritability, withdrawal, and avoidance. For example, a person who lost a loved one right before Christmas may become depressed and irritable during the holiday season. Or, a military veteran may avoid loud noises and bright lights after serving a term of duty. Our triggers are rooted in painful events from our history. Our brains search for sensations that might suggest a threat in order to protect us from further injury. This means that we may sometimes overreact to seemingly harmless stimuli. However, we can learn to recognize and manage our triggers with the help of emotional regulation.

Changing our reaction

When we are triggered, we may withdraw, feel hurt or angry, and react aggressively. This is because we are fighting off a painful emotion that has been brought up. For example, if someone says to us, "You're not smart enough to apply for that job," we may become triggered and feel inadequate. However, if we challenge the negative thought and remind ourselves that we are capable, we will no longer be in a triggered state. The wounds that cause our emotional triggers need to be healed. These negative thoughts are not based in reality, but rather on our *fears* and *insecurities*. We don't want to be triggered all the time, especially if we are empaths, as it can be draining and distressing. So, how can we shift our response? We can start by gently examining and shifting any ingrained negative thoughts, such as "I'm not good enough" or "I'm too sensitive". We also need to address the aspects of ourselves that feel imperfect or harbor self-doubts, such as our body image or our suitability as a potential spouse. When we heal the underlying trauma or faulty beliefs, we liberate ourselves. We won't be as easily triggered or drained.

While we don't choose our reactions, we do have a say in what happens next. Even when we are triggered, we can choose to focus on our own state of being. The most important thing is to direct our attention away from the trigger and towards something positive. For example, we can take a few deep breaths, remind ourselves of our strengths, or visualize ourselves succeeding. We often blame the other person or the outside event for our triggered reactions. However, we need to train ourselves to recognize that the intensity of our reactions is *not* caused by the triggering event. In reality, we may or may not need to react to the actual event that set us off. When triggered, we cannot judge the situation correctly or even take action. It is possible to develop self-regulation skills that reduce the damage caused by our actions. In fact, it is an essential discipline for everyone who wants to make the world a better place. So how do we do that?

Successfully managing our emotional triggers usually requires 4 sets of interventions:

Mindfulness	Distress Tolerance
It trains us to think of our emotions as wildfire that we can control. We can learn to recognize our emotions before they get out of hand and stop fixating on thoughts that only make things worse.	Don't be afraid to feel your feelings! Instead of ignoring them, we can learn to embrace them as a source of information and growth. Face them head-on and learn from them.
Emotion Regulation Training	**Interpersonal Effectiveness**
It teaches us how to manage unpleasant emotions and regulate emotions when they become intense or persistent.	It helps us to manage triggers by making direct changes to our relationships. This is an effective way of controlling strong emotions.

Mindfulness

Mindfulness skills help us balance our emotions, thoughts, and behaviors. They empower us to have mastery over our mind rather than being at its mercy. This is achieved by learning to stay present, developing greater awareness of our thoughts, and shifting focus from stressful to calm things.

Being mindful is like holding a torch in a pitch-black space and shining it where you choose. The skill of mindfulness is the ability to train our mind and present-moment awareness to focus on what we deem helpful. It is the ability to "control the torch" and focus on things that will help us be at ease with what is.

Here are 5 mindfulness exercises to feel more grounded and calmer when navigating an emotional storm:

Inhale calm, exhale stress

Our breathing pattern provides a wealth of information about our mental state. When we are angry or anxious, our breath will likely feel short and shallow. Deep breathing through the diaphragm can help to release stress. When we are disoriented, confused, or overwhelmed, taking long, deep breaths can help to calm the nervous system and bring awareness to the present. This develops a sense of connection with the body. You can try the four-count method if you have never practiced deep breathing. Inhale for four seconds, then exhale for the same amount of time. Repeat this five times. As you inhale, imagine calm pervading every cell of your body, and as you exhale, visualize all your anger being drawn out of your body.

Morning pages

When you wake up, reach for your journal and free-write for three pages. Write whatever comes to mind without editing yourself. Just let it flow. This mind-clearing, introspective exercise allows you to better process your feelings and understand your experience.

My safe place

Visualize a time when you felt calm, safe, or at your best self. Imagine how that safe place makes your body feel. Start to notice how you float away from the stressed situation to safety. Notice how this makes you feel increasingly joyful and calm. Pay attention to your bodily sensations and stay focused on the positive emotions. How about you describe your safe place?

_____

_____

_____

_____

_____

_____

Grounding technique

Bring yourself into the present and feel calmer by getting in touch with your senses. Focus on the following:

5 things you can see _____

4 things you can touch _____

3 things you can hear _____

2 things you can smell _____

and 1 thing you can taste _____

Self-soothing

When triggered, we are like a young child or a frightened animal. We can use self-soothing techniques to calm down. This could include taking a hot bath, listening to gentle music, or lying on the ground.

Distress Tolerance

Distress tolerance skills can help us manage our emotions during a crisis. These skills help us accept reality and cope with our emotions, even when we don't know what we want or need. These crisis-survival skills are short-term coping strategies that help control emotional suffering and prevent destructive actions. For example, people may engage in self-harming acts, run away from the situation, drink alcohol, use drugs, or deny the presence of the stressor in an attempt to stop feeling intense emotional agony. However, these behaviors can have serious long-term effects. By learning distress tolerance skills, we can reduce the intensity and duration of our emotional suffering.

Let us look at some of those skills:

Weigh the pros and cons

When we're in a crisis, our bodies and minds go into fight-or-flight mode. This can make us take irrational decisions that we later regret. It's important to pause and think logically before we act. Making a list of pros and cons of our reaction can help us see the logic and make better decisions.

Radical acceptance

Radical acceptance is the practice of accepting things as they are, without trying to change them. This can be difficult, but it can help to reduce anxiety and distress. To put it simply, *things are what they are.* When we try to control things that are out of our control, we only make ourselves more upset. Acceptance allows us to move forward smoothly without getting emotionally stuck.

Temperature with cold water

The cold temperature of water can shock the body and help to bring you back to the present moment. If you are having trouble controlling your emotions, try taking a cold shower, splashing cold water on your face, or holding ice cubes in your hands. These tasks will not harm you, but they will make it difficult to stay in a heightened emotional state.

STOP

STOP is an acronym that can be expanded as follows:

S: Stop! Don't respond to the trigger. Take control of your body and emotions. Stay still.

T: Take a step back. Remove yourself from the situation. Pause for a moment to breathe deeply. Avoid making snap decisions guided by irrational thoughts.

O: Observe. Take some time to observe your inner and outer environment. What are you thinking? What are you feeling?

P: Proceed mindfully. Consider your goals in the situation and move forward with emotional awareness. What step must you take next to improve the situation, and what kind of action might worsen things?

Distraction

When everything else fails, distraction can be a helpful coping mechanism. While we may like to think that we can multitask, our working memory can only hold so much information at once. If we're feeling overwhelmed, it can be helpful to put the problem on hold and focus on something else until we can come back to it calmly. Distraction can involve physically removing ourselves from the situation or engaging in an activity like talking on the phone, reading a book, or playing with pets.

Emotion Regulation Training

Self-regulation is the ability to pause between our feelings and our reactions. It allows us to take a moment to reflect on a situation before acting. For example, a student who punches their peers and yells at others for trivial reasons is likely to have less emotional control than a student who first notifies the teacher about their difficulties before hitting or yelling. We often say or do things we don't mean when we don't take the time to calm down and collect ourselves. This is because when we react impulsively, we are not thinking clearly. We are simply reacting to whatever is happening in the moment. Self-control and appropriate regulation allow us to remain composed under pressure and keep ourselves from acting unethically. Here are some skills that help regulate emotions:

Self-awareness

Understanding and recognizing our emotions is a crucial first step toward emotional control. For example, if you are feeling lousy, ask yourself, "Am I feeling sad, hopeless, humiliated, or anxious?" Explore your emotions and give yourself some space to feel them. Try to identify the specific emotions that you are experiencing at that very moment and write them down. There is no need to take action or evaluate the causes and effects of your emotions right now. All that is required is to be fully aware of each feeling without judgment.

Reframing the story we tell ourselves

Changing our perspective is a key step in managing our emotions. We can do this by trying to see a difficult situation from a new angle. For example, if we believe that our boss dislikes us, we could try to see the situation from their perspective. Perhaps they are just having a bad day, or they are stressed about a project. By changing our perspective, we can see that the situation is not as bad as we thought, and we can respond in a more constructive way.

Self-compassion

Creating daily self-care time is a great way to improve emotional control. Taking time for ourselves to relax, reflect, and appreciate our strengths can help us to respond to our emotions in a more constructive way. Some simple self-compassion practices include regular journaling, relaxation techniques, and using daily positive affirmations.

Adaptability

Taking a third-person perspective is a great exercise to build adaptability. When we are feeling overwhelmed by complicated emotions that we want to avoid, it can be helpful to think about what our best friend might be going through in this situation. What advice would we give them? We can write down our responses in a journal, and then consider whether we would use the same techniques for ourselves.

Attention control

The goal is to change our focus from unpleasant feelings and enable us to view things positively. For example, instead of feeling uncontrollable rage and guilt after being insulted or abused by someone, we can try to see the situation as a lesson that teaches us to avoid forming relationships with impolite people. By focusing on the lessons we learned from the conflict, we can spare ourselves the intense stress and suffering, and we can also gain insights into how to prevent similar interpersonal disputes in the future.

Interpersonal Effectiveness

Interpersonal effectiveness is the ability to get people to fulfill your needs, carry out your requests, and respect your perspectives. It can improve existing relationships, create fulfilling new connections, and end toxic or dysfunctional relationships. However, our emotions and automatic negative thoughts can often interfere with finding new relationships or ending toxic ones.

The DEARMAN skill is a communication technique that can help us form healthy interpersonal relationships. It stands for:

Describe: Describe the current situation and stick to the facts. Explain to the person what exactly you are reacting to.

Express: Express your emotions and thoughts about the situation without assuming the other person knows how you feel.

Assert: Assert yourself by expressing your needs and wants clearly and confidently. Others do not always know what we want, so we must remind ourselves that others cannot read our minds.

Reward: Reward the person beforehand. Explain the benefits of getting what you want or need. You may also share the harmful effects of not getting what you want or need.

Mindfully: Mindfully focus on your goals. Do not get off-topic. If the other person attacks with comments, threats, or tries to change the subject, ignore them and focus on making your point.

Appear: Appear confident and competent. Make good eye contact.

Negotiate: Negotiate and be willing to give. Look for alternative solutions that will work for everyone involved.

Putting it all together

On the next page, you will find a toolkit to help you identify and manage your triggers.

It is time to put principles into practice and turn inward for some self-reflection. Let's get started!

Managing Triggers Toolkit

Exercise #1 Listing down triggers

Make a list of things that trigger you. These are the external events that cause you to react in an intensely emotional way, often out of proportion. A trigger can also be an absence of behavior. For example, "My husband never thanks me." Make sure that your triggers are observable events, not your interpretations of those events.

_____

_____

_____

_____

_____

_____

_____

_____

_____

_____

_____

_____

Exercise #2 Digging Deep

You can imagine trigger as a 6-story building. The top floor is our immediate reaction to the triggering event. Beneath this initial reaction is a deeper, often more vulnerable emotion. There are also several other floors below, each with a richer, more difficult-to-access emotional or bodily sensation. Finally, we reach the basement, where there is often a core trauma or wound that dates back to our early years. We desperately try to avoid feeling this wound, which is so tender and painful. Our brain is triggered by this wound, causing it to interpret it as a life-or-death situation and start the fight-or-flight response. The first injury is what fuels the entire cycle of being triggered.

Here is an example:

The trigger	Someone found faults in my work.
Initial reaction	I got defensive and denied it.
2nd floor down	My stomach felt tight, and I felt anxious. "Did I spoil everything?" I thought.
3rd floor down	If they were correct, I'm not good at my work.
4th floor down	If I'm not good at what I do, I'm not worthy.
5th floor down	If I'm not worthy, then I'm not loveable.
Core wound	If I'm unlovable, then *I will be lonely forever.*

Pick 2 of your most significant triggers and dig deep, as shown in the above example.

The trigger	
Initial reaction	
2nd floor down	
3rd floor down	
4th floor down	
5th floor down	
Core wound	

The trigger	
Initial reaction	
2nd floor down	
3rd floor down	
4th floor down	
5th floor down	
Core wound	

Exercise #3 Reframe the story

Once you've identified your core wound, you may notice that you've been telling yourself the same story for most of your life. You can start reframing the story by using affirmations to transform the unpleasant emotion into something positive. For example, you might write down an affirmation that reads, "I am lovable and worthy of belonging, even if I sometimes make mistakes in my work." This affirmation positively reframes the previously stated idea. When you start to believe these affirmations, you begin to alter your thought patterns. And when your thoughts change, your emotions also shift.

_____

_____

_____

_____

_____

_____

_____

_____

2

Should we believe everything we think?

Sometimes, our minds can be our worst prisons

Have you ever wondered what a fantastic tool your brain is? Of course, it can also work against you.

Our brains are incredibly intelligent, which has allowed us to build complex civilizations, advance development, and make notable achievements. However, our brains can also turn against us. Sometimes, our worst enemy is ourselves. For example, have you ever struggled to fall asleep because the same thought keeps running through your mind? Do you constantly think about past situations, filled with *what-ifs* or *regrets*? Do you frequently obsess over imagined future events? These are all signs that you might be overthinking. We give a thought far too much time and attention and when we let our thoughts run wild, it can be damaging to our bodies and mental health.

Our brains generate thousands of thoughts daily. These thoughts come and go, directing us on what to do. No wonder burnout is so common, especially for those who constantly overthink and overwork their brains. As we grow up, we acquire the ability to analyze. Our thinking patterns change as we age and become adults. We become better at picking up on subtleties, solving problems, and predicting the future. We also become better at creating and arranging our thoughts using reasoning, problem-solving, remembering, evaluating, and other abilities we have acquired over time. When we think, we bring our imagination, daydreams, and memories to life.

Overthinking

We all go through phases where we feel like our brains won't shut off. We can't stop wondering what our lives would be like if we could have changed the past. This is called overthinking. Overthinking is when we repeatedly think about the same event or situation to the point where it interferes with our life. It can make us feel stuck or prevent us from moving forward. It can be difficult for us to focus on anything else or to push those thoughts out of our minds. The most significant feature of overthinking is its *lack of productivity.* For example, we might lose sleep or spend hours trying to make a choice and miss a deadline. While stress often arises from overthinking, not all overthinking is bad. For example, it's normal to overthink when we're going through a life transition, such as choosing a college, changing jobs, or getting married. This is because these are important decisions that require careful consideration. However, there are times when overthinking can become excessive. We might obsess over insignificant decisions or constantly replay negative thoughts in our minds. This can lead to anxiety, depression, and other mental health problems. Here are some signs that you might be overthinking:

- Dwelling on past events: Thinking about past events over and over again, even when they are out of your control.
- Regretting made decisions: Thinking about decisions you've made and wishing you had made different ones.
- Replaying your mistakes: Thinking about mistakes you've made and how you could have avoided them.

- Rehashing uncomfortable conversations: Thinking about uncomfortable conversations you've had and how you could have handled them differently.
- Fixating on things you can't control: Thinking about things that are out of your control and worrying about them.
- Visualizing the worst-case scenarios: Thinking about the worst possible outcomes of a situation and worrying about them.
- Analyzing the hidden messages in people's words: Trying to figure out what people really mean when they say things, even when they don't say it explicitly.
- Questioning instead of acting: Thinking about all possible outcomes of a situation before you take action, and then not taking any action at all.

Imagine this situation: you accidentally call your new employer by the wrong name. How would you feel and think? A typical worrier might feel a little embarrassed, plan to apologize the next day, and then forget about it and make dinner. However, an overthinker would replay the mistake over and over again, imagining all sorts of negative outcomes. By four in the morning, they might be imagining being passed over for promotions. This situation has triggered a number of questions in the overthinker's mind, which has exaggerated the entire incident. This scenario may seem unimportant, but it is a great example of how overthinking can affect many aspects of our life. Classic examples of what an overthinking mind does include *dwelling on past events* and *anticipating the worst.*

Cognitive Distortions: Errors in our thought process

Cognitive distortions are habitual errors in thinking that lead people to see reality *incorrectly* and *negatively.* For example, someone might say, "I am the unluckiest person in the entire world."

This is an example of *catastrophizing*, which is the tendency to see things as much worse than they really are. Another example is, "I failed my exam. I'm no good and should just quit school." This is an example of *labeling*, which is the tendency to label ourselves or others in negative ways.

Cognitive distortions are biased perspectives we take on ourselves and the world around us. They are negative, irrational thoughts and beliefs that we unknowingly adopt over time. These thought patterns can be very subtle, making it challenging to identify when they become a regular part of our daily thoughts. We often believe what our minds tell us. After all, who can you believe if you can't trust your brain? Our brains are designed to warn us of danger, attract us to potential mates, and solve challenges daily. However, sometimes we should think critically about what our brain tells us. Our brains are wired to draw links between thoughts, ideas, actions, and results. These links can be made surprisingly easily, whether they are healthy or not. Faulty brain connections can form over time, leading to negative thoughts and emotions. It's important to be aware of these faulty connections and to challenge them when they arise. Admitting that you can be prone to distorted thinking can be terrifying. You might say, "There's no way I'm clinging to irrational beliefs!" However, most people experience cognitive distortions at some point. The ability to recognize and change these flawed thought patterns is important for mental health as they have been demonstrated to be positively linked with symptoms of depression.

Let us look closely at a few types of cognitive distortions. See if you can identify and list examples from your life.

Personalization

Personalization is a cognitive distortion that involves taking things personally or blaming ourselves without any logical justification. For example, we might think that our friend was upset with us because they didn't respond to our text message right away. However, it turned out that they were just busy with work. The truth is that not everything is always about us or related to us.

_____

_____

_____

_____

Catastrophizing

Catastrophizing is a cognitive distortion that involves seeing only the worst possible outcomes of a situation. People who catastrophize often fear or assume the worst, even when there is no evidence to support their predictions. For example, someone might think, "If I fail this test, I will never pass school and be a total failure in life." Or, they might assume that having a terrible headache means they have brain cancer or a fatal disease.

_____

_____

_____

_____

Should Statements

Should statements involve using words like "should," "must," or "ought" to describe how we or others should behave. For example, we might think that we "should" always be on time, or that a self-sufficient person "should" never ask for help. When we hold ourselves or others to these rigid rules, we set ourselves up for failure. After all, no one can always be on time, and even the most self-sufficient people sometimes need help. When we inevitably break these rules, we may feel guilty, ashamed, or disappointed in ourselves.

_____

_____

_____

_____

Overgeneralization

Overgeneralization involves making sweeping generalizations based on a single event or experience. We often use words like "always", "never", "everything", and "nothing" to make these generalizations. For example, after a bad breakup, we might think, "I'm always going to be stuck in meaningless relationships and never find love," or "All boys are commitment-phobic." While it may be true that our single experience has been negative, it's important to remember that it doesn't necessarily mean that all future experiences will be the same.

_____

_____

_____

_____

Blaming

Blaming involves making others responsible for our own emotions. For example, we might say, "You made me feel bad." This type of thinking can lead to feelings of anger, resentment, and helplessness. It is important to remember that we are not always in control of how others behave, but we are always in control of our own thoughts and reactions. When we blame others, we are giving them power over us.

_____

_____

_____

_____

Magnification & Minimization

Minimization is when we dismiss our achievements and accomplishments as insignificant. For example, we might think, "I got promoted at work, but it's probably because of luck." Magnification is when we blow things out of proportion and focus more on the negative aspects. For example, we might think, "My friend and I disagreed, so now our friendship is ruined." Both magnification and minimization are cognitive distortions that involve exaggerating or minimizing the importance of certain events or situations.

_____

_____

_____

_____

Mental Filtering

Mental filtering involves filtering out positive information and focusing only on negative aspects. This can lead to people seeing the world in a negative light and feeling overwhelmed by their problems. For example, someone who is engaging in mental filtering might have a good day at work, but then focus on the fact that their takeout dinner order was messed up. They might ignore all of the positive things that happened during their day and focus solely on the negative.

_____

_____

_____

_____

Black-and-White Thinking

Black-and-white thinking involves thinking in extremes without considering the gray area. This can lead to people seeing the world in a very polarized way, with no room for nuance or complexity. For example, someone might think, "My sister is so beautiful, and I am so ugly," or "If I am not perfect, then I am a total failure." These thoughts are all-or-nothing, and they do not allow for any middle ground.

_____

_____

_____

_____

Heaven's Reward Fallacy

This cognitive distortion involves the expectation that one must be rewarded for hard work and sacrifice. This can lead to people feeling resentful and disappointed when their expectations are not met. For example, someone might think, "I worked so hard on that project, so I deserve a promotion." However, the reality is that there are many factors that contribute to a promotion, and hard work is not always the only factor.

_____

_____

_____

_____

Control Fallacies

Control fallacy involves believing that either we control everything or nothing is under our control. This can lead to two unhealthy extremes:

1. Controlling: When we think we can control everything, we may take responsibility for the pain and happiness of everyone around us. This can lead to feeling stressed, overwhelmed, and resentful.

2. Helplessness: When we feel that we cannot control anything, we may turn into helpless victims feeling as though we have no power to improve the quality of our lives. This can lead to feelings of depression, anxiety, and hopelessness.

_____

_____

_____

_____

The toxic effects of negative thinking

As complexities and competition increase daily, negative thinking has become a common experience. However, it becomes concerning when patterns of negative thoughts and feelings form. These can cause daily activities and productivity to suffer, as every situation will likely be viewed negatively. This can result in high disappointment and depression, affecting your behavior, responses, and relationships. While all people with mental illness have habitual negative thinking, it is important to remember that not everyone suffering from negative thoughts is suffering from mental illness. Nevertheless, let us go through the general effects of negative thoughts:

Feelings of sadness, disappointment, and emptiness	Anxiety and panic attacks	Depending on substances such as cigarettes, alcohol, etc., to cope	Social withdrawal and struggling with loneliness
Low energy and productivity	Low motivation and productivity	Losing interest in things previously enjoyed	Lack of self-care and personal grooming
Changes in sleep	Changes in appetite	Increased self-criticism	Anger outbursts
Excessive crying	Negative body image	Reduced self-confidence	Frequent shifts in mood

The effects of negative thinking can be mild and temporary, but they can soon become intense and long-lasting if the negative thoughts behind them are not challenged. This is where we must utilize our superpower: the ability to change how we see any situation. While it is true that we may not always be able to change the circumstances we find ourselves in, by simply shifting our perspective, we can miraculously transform our entire approach to it and, thus, the outcome. We can think of our perspectives as different-colored sunglasses through which we can view the world in a different light. Never forget that you always have the choice to change your mindset. Here is an example:

Anna makes a mistake while working on her project. She thinks, "I'm so stupid for making this mistake. Why can't I be good at anything? I am a total failure, and I've ruined the entire project." As a result, she feels terrible about herself, leading to disappointment, anger, and self-hatred. She also finds it difficult to try again because she anticipates failing again. However, Anna must realize that she is not as helpless as she sees herself in her mind. She needs to question the rationality of her thoughts and observe them without treating them as facts. For example, she could ask herself, "Am I really stupid for making this mistake? Or is it possible that everyone makes mistakes from time to time?" She could also ask herself, "Why can't I be good at anything? Or is it possible that I am good at some things and not so good at others?"

By challenging her negative thoughts, Anna can start to see herself in a more realistic light. This will help her to feel better about herself and to be more motivated to try again.

The ABC Model

A common error in thinking is believing that *the situation* is to be blamed for how we feel and act. For example, "I drink because my husband is so hard to deal with." However, our *thoughts* about a situation, rather than the situation itself, determine how we feel and act. This is the cornerstone of the ABC model developed by psychologist and researcher, Dr. Albert Ellis. This model is designed to help you identify inaccurate and irrational beliefs and challenge them to explore alternative solutions to a problem.

The ABC model consists of 5 steps in ascending order. See if you can list your examples in the space provided.

Activating Event (A): This is the event that triggers the negative emotion. For example, your husband is late for dinner again. See if you can list your own activating event.

- Prompt #1 What has happened?

- Prompt #2 What did I do?

- Prompt #3 What did others do?

_____

_____

_____

_____

_____

_____

Beliefs (B): These are the thoughts you have about the activating event. It is your interpretation of the event. What thoughts are you having about what just happened? For example, "He doesn't care about me. I'm a terrible wife."

- Prompt #1 What do I believe about my activating event?

_____

_____

_____

_____

_____

_____

_____

Consequences (C): These are the emotions and behaviors that result from the beliefs. For example, you feel angry, hurt, and resentful. You may start to yell at your husband or withdraw from him emotionally.

- Prompt #1 Am I feeling angry, disappointed, frustrated, hurt, etc?

- Prompt #2 Am I behaving in a way that does not work for me?

_____

_____

_____

_____

_____

_____

Disputing (D): This is the process of challenging the irrational beliefs. It is time to *"dispute the beliefs"* and challenge them to create positive consequences. This is where you critically examine the beliefs you wrote down in 'B' and see whether they are realistic and helpful. For example, "Is it really true that he doesn't care about me? Or is it possible that he's just busy?" "Am I really a terrible wife? Or am I just feeling hurt and angry right now?"

- Prompt #1 What is the proof that my beliefs are true?

- Prompt #2 Are my thoughts helpful?

_____

_____

_____

_____

_____

_____

New Beliefs (E): This is the process of developing new, more rational beliefs. For example, "My husband is late sometimes, but that doesn't mean he doesn't care about me. I'm a good wife, and I'm doing the best I can."

- Prompt #1: What new thoughts can I create to replace unhelpful ones?

- Prompt #2 What are my new feelings?

_____

_____

_____

_____

_____

_____

The main message of the ABC model is that while external factors can certainly harm our lives, we have some control over how we respond to the challenges we face. The more constructively we respond, the better our outcomes will be. However, just because someone has a positive attitude doesn't mean they can't get hurt. Instead, it says that a positive attitude can help someone cope with difficult times more effectively.

Journaling for mental clarity and emotional stability

Did you know that the desire to document events of our lives is as old as handwriting itself? While diaries found in early civilizations were mostly kept as public records, the modern diary has its roots in 15th-century Italy, where they were used for accounting. As time passed, diaries began reflecting private life more than public life. Famous late 18th-century writers and artists such as Sylvia Plath, Virginia Woolf, Leo Tolstoy, and Franz Kafka used the diary as a vital part of their creative process. Their works are widely read even today.

In the 1980s, many public-school systems began using journals in English classes and across curriculum. These journals provided a way for students to develop independent thinking skills. Although they were intended to be educational rather than therapeutic, it was discovered that assignments about reflecting on a topic in their journals revealed great information about students' emotional lives. Students also reported feeling relieved of stress and tension after writing down confusing thoughts or feelings.

With the advancement of technology, diaries have gone digital. People began blogging and taking to social media platforms like Facebook, Instagram, and Twitter to share their experiences. Rather than keeping intimate details about life private, people now focused on making them public. Whether the desire is to express or conceal, journaling and documenting have always been widely accepted ways of navigating difficult emotions and thoughts. Multiple types of research in the past few decades have found the benefits of writing down our deepest thoughts and feelings.

So, how does it work? Journaling works on two levels. It deals with both our *thoughts* and *feelings.* It allows us to express our feelings rather than suppress them, which is widely known to be beneficial for our mental health. Many of us secretly harbor heavy emotions, such as hurt and shame, that we haven't shared with others. When we journal, our pain gets an outlet rather than just swarming around in our heads. When we have let out what we were holding back, our minds feel lighter and our hearts calmer. Writing also allows us to make meaning of our experiences. In our minds, things usually appear much more complicated than reality. However, when we write down our thoughts, one by one, we can connect the dots and make a coherent story. We learn to look at our experiences objectively and see them differently. This helps us uncover new things about ourselves and the world. While trauma can shake our beliefs about how life works, writing about it gives us a sense of control.

Journaling, then, is a tool for putting our personal experiences, thoughts, opinions, and feelings into words, which helps us understand and make sense of them. It can be a safe and constructive way, to develop our self-awareness, and to connect with others.

Journaling prompts for releasing difficult emotions

If you need help analyzing what you are experiencing, here are a few prompts.

Anger

Are you feeling aggressive? Maybe you're mad at your sister for forgetting to ask to borrow one of your things again. Do you feel like punching someone? Or perhaps your angry feelings for someone who hurt you came up again. Whatever the case, journaling can help you dig into what is beneath that anger. Here are some prompts to help you analyze your anger:

- "When I feel angry like this, it helps to remember..."
- Write a *no-send letter* (a letter that you will not be sending) to the person who is making you angry and explain why their behavior hurts you.
- What am I hiding behind my anger? How can I use my anger to respond constructively?

Anxiety

Anxiety is a normal emotion that everyone experiences from time to time. However, for some people, anxiety can become overwhelming and debilitating. When we experience anxiety, it is often because we feel a lack of control in the face of uncertainty. This can feel like drowning and struggling to stay afloat.

- Free-write for a set amount of time without stopping to edit or censor your thoughts. Don't worry about spelling or grammar. Just keep going. If some thoughts keep repeating, don't hesitate to keep writing them.

- Describe how you can feel more prepared for the situation and make yourself more comfortable dealing with it. Why not create a list of things that you can control?

- Brainstorm ways to bring calm into your life.

Jealousy

Jealousy is a normal emotion that everyone experiences from time to time. However, when jealousy becomes overwhelming and consumes our lives, it can be destructive to our relationships and our mental health. Journaling can be a helpful way to work through feelings of jealousy. When we journal about our jealousy, we can start to identify the root cause of our feelings. We can also start to challenge the negative thoughts and beliefs that are fueling our jealousy.

- How do you compare yourself to others?

- What are some affirmations or positive self-talk that you can use to counter the feelings of jealousy?

- What are some healthy ways to cope with your jealousy?

Loneliness

It can be common to feel disconnected from others, especially during challenging times. Journaling can be an effective and proactive way to combat this feeling. However, figuring out how to start writing about such a complex feeling can be difficult. Here are some prompts that can help you get started:

- Write about a time when you felt encouraged, cared for, and loved by someone.
- What can you do for someone else right now?
- How do you view yourself in loneliness? Is it an accurate representation of who you are?

Self-loathing

It is common for people to be their own worst critics, judging themselves for how they behave, eat, act, dress, etc. This negative self-talk can very quickly lead to self-hatred. If not brought under control, self-hatred can be detrimental to our well-being and affect our relationships, productivity, and overall quality of life. However, it can be prevented with the help of journaling.

Here are some prompts that can help you journal about your self-hatred:

- What kind of words are you craving to hear from someone you love? Write a letter to yourself as if you are this person, and write down the words you would want to hear.
- What are your favorite things about yourself? Make a list of compliments that you have received from others. What are some of your strengths and qualities that you admire?

Write about a time when you felt most at peace with yourself, even if that was during your childhood. Describe that experience in detail.

Suffering is optional

Our thoughts are not always accurate representations of the world around us. We create stories to explain why things happen the way they do, and these stories can be inaccurate or misleading. When we treat our thoughts as absolute facts, we set ourselves up for unpleasant feelings. *Our thoughts are temporary, and many of them are not valid.* This can be upsetting, but it also empowers us. If we can learn to control how we respond to our thoughts, we can release the thoughts that make us depressed and bring peace into our lives. When we stop believing everything we think, we allow ourselves to be more proactive and live the life we imagine for ourselves. We can let go of the beliefs that bring us pain and focus on appreciating what *is*.

Fact vs opinion

When we are going through challenging times, our emotions and opinions can spiral out of control. Our emotions strengthen our beliefs, which in turn intensify our feelings. To break this cycle, we need to focus on the facts.

One way to do this is to ask ourselves, "Is my thought a fact or just an opinion?" For example, if we see a headline in the newspaper that says, "The economy is in recession," we might ask ourselves if this is actually a fact or just the journalist's opinion. If we find that the thought is just an opinion, we can look at the data to see what we know for sure about the situation.

Here are some examples of facts and opinions:

Facts

- I weigh 90kg.
- My co-worker did not greet me.
- I failed my exam.

Opinions

- I am unattractive due to my weight.
- My co-worker ignored me.
- I am a failure.

Facts cannot be argued or challenged, but opinions can be. There can be multiple opinions about a situation, and our opinion is just one of them. When we change our viewpoints, we change the story we tell ourselves, which can lead to positive emotions.

The opinions above can be positively reframed as follows:

- I am not unattractive due to my weight. I am unique and special, and I am grateful for the love that finds its way to me.
- All I know is that my co-worker did not greet me. Perhaps, she is going through something difficult. I will give her some space and see if she comes around.
- Failing one test does not mean I am a failure. It just means that I need to put in more effort. I will try harder next time.

Now, how about you try some? List down some negative opinions you have been holding onto, and reframe them into positive ones.

_____

_____

_____

_____

3

When anxiety attacks

Go slow and tread with compassion

Anxiety is a word used to describe a range of emotions and physical sensations, from mild discomfort to debilitating fear. While it is an experience that most of us go through, it can be difficult to put into words. Here are three expressions that can help us understand what anxiety feels like:

A hurricane of emotions

"This emotional turmoil within me is like a hurricane, destroying everything in its path. The wind is blowing fiercely, and the rain is beating, and there is nothing I can do to stop it. I can hardly do anything to escape this storm or protect myself from its wrath."

Anxiety can feel like a hurricane, with your mind being flooded with negative thoughts and emotions. This can make it difficult to focus or concentrate, and it can also lead to physical symptoms such as a racing heart or shortness of breath. The wind and rain represent the negative thoughts and emotions that are swirling around in your mind. The emotional storm is so powerful that it feels like you can't escape it, and you may feel like you're going to be swept away.

A monkey on your back

"It feels like a monkey on my back, constantly bugging and weighing me down. I cannot escape its constant chatter. I cannot think clearly or concentrate. The weight of this monkey is becoming unbearable, and I don't think I can last long till I break."

The analogy of a monkey on your back is a helpful way to understand what anxiety feels like. The monkey represents the negative thoughts and emotions that are constantly circling in your mind. The weight of the monkey is a metaphor for the physical symptoms of anxiety, such as racing heart or shortness of breath.

A heavy sensation in your stomach

"It's like this heavy sensation in my stomach. It makes me so suffocated that I can't catch my breath. The more I fight it, the stronger this feeling gets. I am scared, and I fear that I will lose control of myself. I can sense danger, I don't know why, but I can sense that something terrible will happen."

This analogy focuses on the stomach, a visceral organ that is closely linked to our emotions. When we feel anxious, our bodies release stress hormones, which can cause the stomach to feel heavy or upset. The feeling of suffocation is a metaphor for the feeling of being overwhelmed by anxiety. The fear of losing control is a common fear for people with anxiety. The sense of danger is a feeling of dread or foreboding that something bad is going to happen.

What anxiety is NOT

Even if you don't suffer from anxiety, you probably know someone who does. With anxiety being a common mental health condition, you'd think that people would be well-informed about what it is and isn't. However, there are still many misconceptions about it. False information and shame around anxiety can hinder people from seeking care for mental health difficulties, so it is necessary to dispel stereotypes wherever possible. This is why it is so essential for us to truly understand what anxiety is and isn't. Myths and false beliefs about anxiety have far-reaching harmful consequences for those affected, and it is crucial to address those misconceptions with facts. So, let's get into it!

1. It is not just in your head.

Anxiety can also manifest in physical symptoms, especially during panic attacks. The physical symptoms can be so intense that they can be mistaken for a heart attack. Some common physical symptoms of anxiety include sweating, numbness, shortness of breath, and nausea.

2. It is not the same as depression.

Although both are often co-occurring conditions, they are distinct from each other. Anxiety is related to the fear that things will go wrong and make life worse, while depression is characterized by the belief that things are already bad and they can't get better. It is important to not confuse these two conditions, as they can have different treatment approaches.

3. It is not fear.

The primary difference between anxiety and fear is that anxiety is future-oriented, while fear is present-oriented. Fear is a reaction to a real or perceived threat, while anxiety is a feeling of worry or nervousness about something that might happen in the future. For example, if you are being chased by an animal, you would feel fear because there is a real danger present. However, if you are feeling anxious about an upcoming exam, you are not actually in danger, but you are worried about something that might happen.

4. It is not the same as overthinking.

Overthinking is a habit that can lead to anxiety. When negative thoughts spiral out of control, especially those about the future, they can trigger anxious feelings. While overthinking does not have physical symptoms, anxiety does.

5. It is not something to hide.

Anxiety is not your fault. It's important to remember that. Feeling ashamed of anxiety is a common experience, but it's important to challenge that stigma. Mental health conditions are just as real as physical health conditions, and we should not be ashamed of them. It's okay to reach out for help when you're struggling with anxiety. There are many resources available, and you don't have to go through this alone.

So, what IS anxiety?

It is our body's natural response to stress. It is a feeling of nervousness, worry, or unease about what might happen. Excessive worrying can make it difficult to control intrusive thoughts about worst-case scenarios. Anxious thoughts can make it hard for the mind to settle down and relax. Here are some *mood changes* that one can expect when experiencing anxiety:

Feeling restless	**Feeling fidgety**
Feeling fearful	**Feeling on edge**
Feeling impatient	**Feeling nervous**
Feeling frustrated	**Feeling tense**

Along with the above changes, anxiety can also interfere with how our mind functions. Let us look at some *cognitive effects*:

Confusion	Poor memory
Difficulty paying attention	Difficulty speaking
Difficulty being present	Having fearful memories or images
Fear of losing control	Difficulty with being logical

It's common knowledge that anxiety is not just a mental or emotional experience. It kicks a fight-or-flight response which can result in real *physical symptoms* as follows:

Nausea or diarrhea	Racing heart
Dry mouth	Headache
Dizziness or lightheadedness	Muscle tension
Fatigue	Shortness of breath

Anxiety Disorders

Anxiety is a common emotion that everyone experiences from time to time. However, it is only considered a disorder when it causes significant distress or interferes with daily life. *A visit to a mental health professional is a must for correct diagnosis followed by an effective treatment course.* Anxiety disorders can persist over time and often lead to depression if left untreated. Fortunately, anxiety disorders can be treated effectively with therapy or medication. Some of them have been described below:

Generalized Anxiety Disorder

Generalized anxiety disorder (GAD) can develop around the age of 30, but it can also affect children. People with GAD worry excessively and uncontrollably about everyday situations, such as returning a book to the library. They may worry about family, health, or finances, even when there is no reason to. GAD can last for more than 6 months, and people with this disorder may not be able to identify the source of their worry. In mild cases, people with

GAD can function socially and lead meaningful lives. However, in severe cases, they may have difficulty carrying out simple daily activities and may avoid situations due to worry.

Obsessive-Compulsive Disorder

Obsessive-compulsive disorder (OCD) is a mental health disorder characterized by unwanted and intrusive thoughts (*obsessions*) and repetitive behaviors (*compulsions*). People with OCD may have upsetting obsessions, such as a fear of contamination by germs, a fear of injury, or a need to arrange things in specific ways. These obsessions can trigger distressing feelings, and people with OCD may engage in repetitive behaviors, or compulsions, try to eliminate the obsessions. For example, someone who is afraid of contamination by germs may wash their hands repeatedly or avoid touching certain objects. It is important to note that not everyone who experiences obsessive thoughts or compulsive behaviors has OCD. To be diagnosed with OCD, the cycle of obsessions and compulsions must be so severe that it consumes more than an hour per day, causes significant distress, and interferes with important activities.

Phobia

A phobia is an intense and irrational fear of a specific object or situation. This fear is often out of proportion to the actual danger posed by the object or situation. People with phobias may experience a range of symptoms, including anxiety, panic attacks, and avoidance behavior. Common phobias include flying, heights, and injections.

Post-Traumatic Stress Disorder

Post-traumatic stress disorder (PTSD) is a mental health disorder that can develop after someone experiences or witnesses a life-threatening or traumatic event. Common examples of traumatic events that can trigger PTSD include war, natural disasters, major accidents, and physical or sexual abuse. The main features of this disorder include flashbacks of the situation, difficulty sleeping or frequent nightmares, feelings of loneliness, and/or aggressive outbursts. People with PTSD may also avoid related situations and experience intense fear, guilt, sadness, and worry. They may also become jumpy or easily startled.

Social Anxiety Disorder

Social anxiety disorder (SAD) is characterized by a constant, intense, and long-term fear of being watched and judged by others. This fear can lead to avoidance of social situations, which can in turn affect work, school, and other daily activities. If you have been struggling with any of the symptoms of SAD for an extended period, it is helpful to see a therapist. A mental health professional can diagnose SAD and help you develop coping mechanisms.

Habits that make anxiety worse

If you experience anxiety regularly, there is a good chance that you are making mistakes that are making your condition worse. Nobody wants to live with anxiety, but many people with anxiety disorders find themselves repeatedly behaving in ways that undermine their ability to cope with their symptoms. You may be exacerbating your condition without even realizing it. Part of managing your anxiety is learning to avoid common anxiety mistakes and maximizing your ability to cope. So, let's take a look at some habits that can make our anxiety worse.

Sleep Deprivation

Sleep deprivation is one of the most common bad habits that can contribute to anxiety. The stress of anxiety can make it hard to fall asleep, and not getting enough rest can worsen anxiety symptoms. People with anxiety often have trouble sleeping, which can worsen their symptoms. Sleep is one of the most important coping strategies for dealing with stress. Sleep deprivation can increase your stress levels, making it difficult to fall asleep and exacerbating anxiety symptoms. If you find yourself worrying about things that keep you awake, try creating a relaxing bedtime routine that frees you from gadgets and helps you wind down. You can also try journaling to help you process your thoughts and worries before bed. Additionally, daytime physical activity can help you tire your body and reduce your anxiety levels, making it easier to sleep at night. Most importantly, don't intentionally avoid sleep. Getting enough rest is essential for managing stress and anxiety.

Use of stimulant drugs

Another harmful habit that can contribute to anxiety is using stimulants. Stimulants are drugs that excite the mind and body. They can include caffeine, tobacco, and illegal hard drugs. Because drugs place significant stress on your body, they can potentially exacerbate anxiety. It is unclear whether stimulants can cause anxiety on their own, Still, they can certainly worsen anxiety symptoms. In some cases, they can even cause anxiety when taken in excess or during withdrawal. It's important to be aware that caffeine is also found in chocolate, tea, and sodas. If you consume these stimulants frequently, your anxiety will likely increase.

Living a sedentary lifestyle

Exercise is a critical component in treating anxiety. In fact, a lack of exercise may be one of the primary reasons that anxiety rates have risen in recent decades. As people have become more sedentary, they have also become more stressed and anxious. What makes this more difficult is that anxiety can cause you to want to be inactive. However, it is important to find a way to overcome this. If you do not exercise, you will experience increased worry and your coping abilities will decrease significantly.

Victimizing yourself

Another harmful habit is adopting a victim mentality. This happens when you see yourself as a victim of anxiety rather than someone who is capable of overcoming it. One of the most common behaviors that comes from a victim mentality is *moping*. This is when you give in to anxiety and spend most of your time feeling sorry for yourself instead of fighting it. It is important to get outside and avoid letting anxiety control you. Spend time with friends and plan enjoyable activities. Look for ways to laugh. Never allow anxiety to dictate your life.

Watching the news all the time

While it is important to stay informed, obsessively watching the news can increase anxiety. Television news can be anxiety-inducing because of the rapid pace of content delivery, the use of fast-paced music and conversation, and the often-negative visuals. It is rare to hear a positive story on the news, and most stories are about war and violence, which can be triggering for people with anxiety. There are less anxiety-inducing ways to stay informed. The best solution is to limit your exposure to the news and read it in small doses. This way, you can control what and how quickly you consume news, which can help you stay informed without feeling overwhelmed.

Spending too much time checking social media

We all want to stay connected with our friends and see the latest memes, but there can be a cost to engaging on social media. Have you ever checked Instagram for a minute, only to find yourself two hours later wondering where the time went and feeling anxious?

Excessive social media use can increase anxiety in a number of ways. You may be exposed to a lot of negative news articles at once, which can leave you feeling powerless, sad, and worried about the state of the world. You may be comparing yourself and your life to the seemingly perfect moments of your friends or even celebrities on social media, which can lead to feelings of inadequacy. You may also spend more time on social media than you intended, taking away from more productive activities.

While it's okay to check Instagram and Facebook throughout the day, it's important to be mindful of your mental health. Set a 15-minute timer for yourself, and when it goes off, you're done for the day. It's also important to schedule *white space* in your calendar. This time is sacred and should be used to relax, rest, and give your brain a break. Treat this white space as seriously as you would any other appointment.

Asking others for reassurance

While it is perfectly okay to seek advice from friends or family, it is important to be aware of when you are seeking reassurance over every little issue. Asking others to tell you that you look fine or that whatever you are worried about won't happen is a common anxiety response. However, in the long run, this can actually worsen anxiety. While it may temporarily decrease anxiety, you will need reassurance to deal with it the next time you worry about something. This turns what may seem like harmless behavior into a habit that is difficult to break. For some people, it can dramatically worsen their anxiety.

Panic attacks

A panic attack is a sudden surge of intense fear and worry that can cause physical and psychological symptoms. The fear is often *irrational* and *disproportionate* to the situation or event that triggered the attack. While anyone can have a panic attack, repeated or ongoing attacks may be a sign of a panic or anxiety disorder that requires treatment. The physical symptoms of a panic attack can mimic those of a heart attack or other medical emergency. They may also accompany a fear of death. These symptoms often develop suddenly and can occur in a calm or anxious state. Panic attacks typically last between 5 and 20 minutes, with the peak of symptoms occurring within 10 minutes. They can happen multiple times in a few hours, and for some people, they occur every day or once a week.

Many people experience fearful thoughts during panic attacks, such as believing they are having a heart attack, stroke, or going crazy. Some people are afraid of losing control or fainting during an attack, while others worry that the attack will never end. These thoughts can make you more alert, making it more likely for another episode to occur. During an attack, these terrifying thoughts can also make the experience more intense and distressing.

But why do panic attacks happen in the first place? Studies have shown that people who experience frequent panic attacks have high anxiety sensitivity. This means that they are fearful of the symptoms of anxiety itself. They are too aware of their bodies and constantly checking to make sure everything is okay. While it is normal to experience changes in our physical sensations throughout the day, people with high anxiety sensitivity can misunderstand these normal physical signs as threatening and trigger a panic attack.

Some people believe they are at an increased risk of developing physical or mental illnesses. Perhaps they had a history of physical illnesses as a child, lost a loved one to a heart attack, or had a family member who struggled with cancer. As a result, they may misinterpret anxiety or panic symptoms as a sign of a heart attack, going crazy, or fainting. People who have these kinds of concerns are also more likely to experience anxiety.

Alternatively, specific situations can become associated with panic attacks in people who have frequent panic attacks. For example, someone might have been driving on the highway to a job interview when they became anxious and had a panic attack. As a result, people may associate highway driving with panic attacks and fear of losing control and causing accident. This fear may cause people to avoid driving on the highway altogether.

If you experience panic attacks, it is important to seek professional help. A therapist can help you understand your anxiety and develop coping mechanisms to manage it. Medication can also be helpful in reducing the frequency and severity of the panic attacks.

The power of affirmations

An affirmation is a positive statement that is typically focused on oneself. It is a way of promoting change and self-love while reducing worry and fear. Affirmations can be helpful in changing subconscious thoughts. When you hear something supportive and encouraging, it often increases the likelihood that you will act in ways that make your affirmations a reality.

Affirmations can help you feel good about yourself by improving how you view yourself and strengthening your belief in your ability to achieve your goals. They can also help to reduce worry, tension, and self-doubt that often accompany anxiety. When anxious thoughts take control and make it difficult to focus on more positive possibilities, affirmations can help you regain control and change your mental habits.

However, affirmations cannot suddenly remove anxiety. They can help you develop and reinforce new attitudes and behaviors, but they are not a magic bullet. If you are struggling with anxiety, it is important to seek professional help in addition to using affirmations.

Creating your own affirmations

Start with "I" or "My"

A first-person perspective might help you connect your affirmations with your sense of self more deeply. This makes them more relevant to your goals and easy to believe.

Always keep your affirmations in the present tense

If you write them in the future tense, they will have minimal effect on your current behavior. Instead, frame your affirmation as if it were already true. This will strengthen the possibility that you will act in ways that make it true. For example, "I am confident and can talk to strangers comfortably," or "I feel happy and content."

Choose a negative thought and write its positive opposite

For example, if you feel lonely, you could try repeating to yourself, "I am loved, and love surrounds me in different forms." Similarly, if you are struggling with body image issues, it may help to think, "I am beautiful, and my body is perfect. I am loved by myself and others unconditionally."

Don't use "I want" or "I need"

When we use these words, we are unconsciously telling ourselves that we are lacking something, which can make us feel disappointed and less content with our lives. Instead, we should frame our affirmations as an expression of gratitude for already possessing and being what we desire and want. For instance, we could say, "I am exactly where I need to be, and everything works out for the greater good."

Affirmations for mitigating anxiety

When you sense anxiety building, try repeating below-given affirmations while practicing deep breathing or any other relaxation technique that works for you.

I can handle this. I am in control.	I calm my thoughts. I am serene.
All is well with me. I am safe and relaxed.	I believe in my ability to cope. I trust myself.
I accept this feeling. It is just anxiety.	I don't have to do this alone. I can ask for help.
Every cloud has a silver lining, and I trust the universe.	I can pause and breathe and show my body that I am safe.
I am grateful for the blessings in my life. I love and approve of myself.	It is safe to let go. I accept life – past, present, and future.

Managing anxiety

If you have ever experienced extreme anxiety, you know how it may affect your entire existence. Fear and thoughts about future disasters can overwhelm your mind. As your fight-or-flight response sets in, your body will tighten. You may also feel spiritually tired as your energy is depleted by this inner turmoil. Because anxiety can take so many forms, any single strategy for dealing with it is unlikely to be enough. It takes a broader approach to tackle the various aspects of our anxious experience. Our well-being depends on the simple practices of minding our thoughts, facing our fears, and being present.

Change the story

Anxiety constantly creates stories about the future, which we often mistake for reality. For example, it might say, "I'm going to fail," and we accept that as a fact. However, these negative predictions are not facts in the same way that weather forecasts are not weather. When we start paying attention to what our minds are doing, we will notice that they are a reliable source of fake news. They are great at generating stories about all the things that will go wrong: you won't be on time, you'll let everyone down, you'll get sick, your loved ones are in danger, or disaster is about to strike.

When we recognize anxious thoughts as stories, we can start to question their truthfulness. Are our assumptions the only possible outcome, or could there be other possibilities we're not considering? When we worry about something terrible happening today, we can ask ourselves how likely that scenario is. Has it happened before? Is it the most likely scenario? Could anything else happen instead?

Most of the time, we tend to worry about things that are unlikely to happen. As a result, our anxiety causes us unnecessary pain. Instead, we can redirect our energy to the things around us that we do have control over.

Face your fears

Anxiety pushes us to avoid what we fear, but avoidance increases our fear. The more we avoid, the more we strengthen the idea that what we're afraid of is actually dangerous. For example, if we avoid certain social situations because we're worried that people will be judgmental, we'll reinforce our fear of those situations.

Avoidance is also addictive, leading to even more avoidance. When we avoid something that causes us anxiety, we experience relief, which our brain interprets as a reward. This reward increases the likelihood that we'll avoid it again. Our world shrinks, and we miss out on great experiences. We may also see ourselves as inadequate to face life's challenges. Nothing conquers anxiety as powerfully as facing what we're afraid of. When we stop avoiding, we give our brain a chance to learn something new. We'll likely discover that our feared disasters don't come true. Instead, we'll find manageable problems that we can handle. Look for ways you have let fear hold you back – at work, in your relationships, or in your free time. Face one of your fears today by choosing something somewhat challenging yet manageable. Reach out to someone you trust for support if necessary. Imagine your life if you pushed through one fear every day.

Be present

Anxiety is caused by thoughts about the future. Therefore, focusing on the present moment can be an effective way to reduce anxiety. Anxiety does not exist when we are fully present in the moment. This is not to say that there are no challenges in the present. In fact, life can be viewed as a series of challenges that we must overcome. However, we can manage these challenges using our skills and experience in the present moment. There is no difference between anxiety and actual difficulties. In most cases, what we fear does not actually happen, or it is not as bad as we imagined it would be. For example, someone who is afraid of giving a speech may find that the experience is unpleasant, but it is manageable.

Putting it all together

On the next page, you will find a toolkit to help you manage your anxiety by challenging negative thoughts. Knowledge is nothing without application, so let's turn inward for some self-reflection. Let's get started!

Exercise #1

Consider a thought about the future that causes you anxiety. If you think that what you are imagining is likely to happen, or you worry that it would still be horrible if it did happen, write your thought on the left below. Formulate it as a statement, for example, "I will lose my job" or "We will break up." Then, write the answers to the questions listed here on the right side.

- Would it be terrible if this happened?
- What are the consequences of this happening?
- How will I cope if it does occur?
- Would I be affected by this forever, or would I ultimately get over it?

Thought (Prediction)	Answers to the questions listed above (Rational Response)

Exercise #2

This exercise aims to distinguish between different types of negative events. We can learn that not all unpleasant situations are equally serious. This awareness itself can be enough to reduce our anxiety.

Have you ever thought, "I know it's unlikely, but if it did happen, would it really be terrible?" It can be quite useful to examine a potentially difficult situation more deeply to evaluate how bad the event would be and how we would react if it occurred. Let us rate different types of distressing situations to measure how catastrophic these events would be if they happened. Rate each of these occurrences from 1 to 5 in terms of how difficult it would be to cope with the event:

1 – I would have no trouble coping at all.

2 – I would have to face a few bad days as a result, but would recover pretty quickly.

3 – I would take substantial time to recover, but I would surely recover.

4 – I would be impaired for a while.

5 – I would fall apart, go crazy, and would never recover.

_____ Argument with a loved one

_____ Death of a loved one

_____ Heard someone say mean things about you

_____ Failed a test

_____ _____ (insert your own)

_____ _____ (insert your own)

_____ _____ (insert your own)

4

More than sad:
The anatomy of depression

Remember, it never rains forever

Thousands of people around the world suffer from sadness or depression at some point in their lives. Sadness is a normal human emotion that occurs during stressful or upsetting moments. Many life experiences can cause us to feel sad or miserable. The death of a loved one, divorce, job loss, financial difficulties, or domestic problems can all have a negative impact on our mood. Failure on a test or being turned down for a job are just a few of the many situations that can cause sadness. It is an emotion that always has a *trigger*. Although it usually fades away with time, we can usually find some relief by crying, venting, or talking about our problems.

If this feeling does not go away or we are unable to resume normal function, it could be sign of a mental health disorder known as *depression*. If our poor mood worsens or lasts for more than 2 weeks, we should see a mental health professional who will help us gain insight into our condition. Understanding the difference between depression and sadness can help us process both in a healthy way.

Sadness is a natural response to disappointment, failure, and loss. It can lead people to look inward, find meaning in their experiences, and move on. While sadness resolves on its own, depression is a persistent illness that often requires treatment. It is a serious mental health disorder that can have a significant impact on many aspects of a person's life. It can make it difficult to even get through the day. It comes on like a thick cloud, without any apparent cause, and drains energy, motivation, meaning, and self-worth.

The term *depression* has been used so often in recent years that it has lost its meaning and spirit. People often use it to describe feeling sad, down, or unmotivated. However, depression is a serious mental illness that can have a profound impact on a person's life.

Here are some examples of how the term *depression* is often misused:

- "I'm so depressed today that I don't feel like doing anything." This statement is often used to describe feeling tired, unmotivated, or bored. However, it is not accurate to say that someone is depressed simply because they are feeling down.
- "This place is so depressing." This statement is often used to describe a place that is dark, dreary, or uninviting. However, it is not accurate to say that a place is *depressing* simply because it is not aesthetically pleasing.
- "Why are you so quiet? Are you depressed?" This question is often asked of people who are not talking or socializing. However, there are many reasons why someone might be quiet, and depression is not always the reason.
- "Cheer up, don't be so depressed." This statement is often used to try to make someone feel better. However, it can be invalidating and unhelpful to tell someone who is struggling with depression to simply *cheer up*.

Social media and television have made the term *depression* very widespread and casual. It is often used to describe many feelings, such as sadness, grief, sorrow, loneliness, melancholy, unhappiness, gloominess, and so on. This casual use of words related to mental disorders as supplements for temporary feelings of worry and sadness is widespread today.

This is because many people use exaggerations and superlatives to make a point and be taken seriously. They fail to understand that they are doing so by harming those who are suffering from these disorders. These people regard mental illness as a choice rather than something unavoidable or uncontrollable. This is often followed by the suicide of the sick person and denial by loved ones who repeatedly brush away their condition, refusing to recognize it for what it is. This is why it is critical to recognize the difference between *depression* and *sadness*. We must unite to challenge society's habit of trivializing mental disorders, especially depression. We must educate people about the difference between sadness and depression, and we must destigmatize mental illness so that people who are struggling can get the help they need.

Depression is caused by a combination of factors, including genetics, brain chemistry, and life experiences. Sad hormones in our bodies naturally last longer than their happy equivalents. As a result, some mental trauma can trigger sadness, causing the brain to fall into a habit of releasing more hormones that promote depression by changing the way that the mind functions. If left untreated, depression can worsen over time. It is not as simple as thinking positively. To reverse this, it takes a lot of external assistance.

To make matters worse, depression is not just a feeling that goes away after a few weeks or months. Not acknowledging this condition can delay the recovery process and force someone who needs help and a positive environment to suffer in silence. For example, those who are sad after going through a breakup have every right to feel the way they do. No one with depression would invalidate their feelings, because they would understand the pain. The main difference is that people with depression feel this way even when there is no clear reason. Another difference is that people with depression do not go up to others who suffer from it and say, "It's just a matter of willpower." That's usually what someone who carelessly uses the term would do.

What does depression look like?

Depression can be seen as a cave, and coming out of it can be a long and challenging process. Not everyone who has depression exhibits all of its symptoms. Some people have a few symptoms, while others have many. The degree and intensity of symptoms will differ among people and over time. However, if any of the following symptoms persist for more than 2 weeks, it is important to consult a mental health professional.

Feeling hopeless about the future	Feeling helpless and lonely	Feeling worthless about oneself	Having thoughts about dying
Excess weight gain or weight loss	Difficulty falling or staying asleep	Not feeling motivated	Lack of self-care and personal grooming
Lack of self-esteem	Changes in sex drive	Self-hatred	Negative body image
Anxiety	Crying spells	Social withdrawal	Overthinking
Long lasting sadness	Mood swings and anger outbursts	Physical aches and pains	Feelings of guilt
Dependency on substances	Low energy and fatigue	Loss of interest in enjoyable activities	Lack of focus and concentration

Although depression is in many ways a baffling and poorly understood disorder, there is growing recognition that it involves many body systems. The condition might have long-lasting effects on brain function, making new episodes likely. Depression can change the way the brain functions, making it more likely that you will experience another episode of depression in the future. Apart from the degree of emotional agony and despair, the longer a depressive episode lasts, the more likely a future recurrence. The length of a depressive episode is an important factor in predicting whether or not you will experience another episode. If you have a depressive episode that lasts for more than two weeks, you are more likely to experience another episode in the future.

However, various treatment options are available for depression, and some of the most effective, particularly in cases of mild to moderate severity, do not require a prescription or any medical intervention unless there are complications. The irony of sadness is that it drains mental energy and makes people feel uninterested or incapable of doing anything, resulting in avoidance. Depression can be a very draining condition. It can make it difficult to focus, concentrate, and make decisions. It can also make you feel like you don't have the energy to do anything. This can lead to avoidance, which can make depression worse. Talking about feelings and thoughts with a qualified therapist can help people regain control of their mental lives and discover healthy perspectives.

Smiling depression

Most people imagine depression as a sad person who can't stop crying, appears exhausted, doesn't want to socialize, and has stopped caring for their health or appearance. However, depression doesn't always look like this. It can also present as an A student, a social butterfly, or an accomplished individual. The most put-together, on-top-of-everything, enthusiastic, and gregarious person could also be depressed. But how could someone be depressed without showing any symptoms? This is known as *smiling depression*.

Depression is often associated with sadness, lethargy, and hopelessness – someone who can't get out of bed. However, how the disorder manifests itself can vary from person to person. *Smiling depression* refers to someone who is depressed on the inside but appears perfectly happy or content on the outside. Their public persona is often "put together," even if some might label it "normal" or "perfect". It is not uncommon for people to keep their depression a secret. There are many personal and professional reasons why people may not disclose their symptoms of sadness and may cover it with a smile, ranging from wanting to keep their personal information private to fearing judgment by others. Here are some of the reasons why people hide their depression:

Fear of burdening others

Depression and guilt often go hand-in-hand. This is because people with depression often feel like they are a burden to others, and they don't want to add to anyone else's problems. This stands especially true for people who are used to taking care of others, rather than being taken care of. They may not know how to ask for help, so they keep their problems to themselves.

Embarrassment

Depression is often misunderstood as a weakness of character or a flaw in one's personality. Some people may even believe that they should be able to *snap out of it* if they are feeling down. However, if they are unable to do so, they may start to think that something is wrong with them. As a result, they may feel embarrassed about their sadness and believe that they should be able to cope with it independently.

Denial

Smiling depression is a situation in which a person appears happy and well-adjusted on the outside, but is secretly struggling with feelings of sadness, hopelessness, and worthlessness. People with smiling depression often put on a brave face and try to hide their true feelings from others. They may feel like they have to be "strong" or "perfect" all the time, and they may be afraid of being judged or rejected if they show their true selves. Denial is a common defense mechanism that people use to cope with difficult emotions. People with smiling depression may deny their condition because they are afraid of what it means to be depressed. They may think that it is a sign of weakness or failure, or they may be afraid of the stigma associated with mental illness.

Fear of retaliation

People with depression may be concerned about the emotional and professional consequences of disclosing their mental health condition. They may worry that they will be judged, stigmatized, or penalized for being depressed. For example, a comedian or a lawyer may be concerned that their employer will question their ability to do their job if they know about their depression. Someone else may be concerned that revealing their depression will cause their partner to leave them. As a result, they may choose to hide their depression behind a smile, in order to avoid risking these negative consequences.

Concerns about appearing weak

People with smiling depression often fear that if they reveal their depression, others will take advantage of them. They may be concerned that others will see them as weak or vulnerable, and that they will be used or manipulated. They may also worry that others will use their depression against them, for example by spreading rumors or gossiping about them. As a result, they may choose to put on a strong front and hide their true feelings.

Guilt

Depression is often accompanied by feelings of guilt. People with depression may feel like they should not be depressed, especially if they have a good life or if they have other people who are struggling more than them. They may believe that they are doing something wrong or that they are to blame for their depression. This can lead to feelings of shame and isolation, which can make it even harder to cope with depression.

Unrealistic thoughts about happiness

Social media can portray happiness in an unrealistic way. People often see photos of happy people on social media, which can make them feel like they are the only ones who are struggling with mental health challenges. This can lead to feelings of isolation and shame, which can make it even harder to cope with mental illness.

Perfectionism

Perfectionists often have a strong need to appear flawless. This means masking any discomfort or troubles they face, even if it means pretending to be happy when they are not. Admitting to depression would mean admitting that their lives are not perfect, which can be very difficult for perfectionists to do.

Smiling depression can be a "fake it till you make it" mindset to depression. The person may assume that by smiling, laughing, and going about their daily activities as if everything were fine, they might finally force themselves to feel okay. In some cases, this can be an effective tactic. This is sometimes referred to as "as if" in therapy. For example, if you want to become more confident, you can act confidently by doing what a confident person would do in a given setting, such as introducing yourself to a stranger at a party or openly discussing your accomplishments and skills at a job interview. Acting "as if" typically works in these situations. Acting happy when you're feeling down or having a bad day can also help – if you smile enough, you will eventually lift your mood.

However, there are times when faking it or acting as if it does not work. It takes more than merely looking happy to induce happiness in people suffering from chronic, long-term depression. Faking it also does not work when the person does it more for the sake of others than oneself. Acting happy to please others or make them feel better can be isolating. That sense of isolation can make depression worse.

Smiling depression can be deceptive. While people with smiling depression appear to be living happily ever after, they still suffer from all of the adverse effects of depression. Smiling depression can lead to various health problems, self-harming behaviors, and even suicide. Compared to other types of depression, which tend to leave sufferers exhausted, smiling depression may put sufferers at a higher risk of suicide because they are less likely to receive help and support and have the energy to act on their suicidal thoughts. Recognizing small indicators of smiling depression can help ensure the sufferer gets the necessary treatment. Even though your condition appears bleak and you question if you can endure another minute of feeling this horrible, there are solutions to get through it and feel better. You are not alone in this scenario.

People who harm themselves often believe that their problems are unbearable and unsolvable. It seems as if nothing they have tried has or will change their situation. Their emotional distress can distort their thinking, making it difficult to trust, understand possible solutions to difficulties, or connect with the love and support that is available to them. Even though you feel like you can't take another minute, remember that feeling does not last forever, especially at an intense level. Suicidal thoughts can become strong, especially if you have used drugs or alcohol. It is critical not to use non-prescription medications, especially if you are depressed or having thoughts about dying.

Some of the thoughts a person who is contemplating dying might have are as follows:

1. "I don't have any other options."
2. "My friends and family will be better off without me."
3. "The only way to end my guilt is to die."
4. "I can't escape my pain."
5. "My death will be my revenge."

What can you do to decrease thoughts about dying?

Problem-solve

It is always beneficial to consider other solutions to ending your life. One way to do this is to list down all the problems you are currently dealing with in your life. Once you have a list of your problems, you can start to brainstorm possible solutions. You can ask for help from someone you love and trust, or you can do some research online. Dealing with one or two minor issues can help to put a stop to suicidal thoughts. When you think more clearly, you can tackle more significant issues.

For example, if you are experiencing the end of a relationship, talking to friends about your pain and hurt might be helpful. You could also get help from a counselor or a crisis helpline, or you could join a social group. There are many resources available to help you cope with difficult times, and you don't have to go through this alone.

Think of reasons to live

Most people who consider suicide want to end their suffering, but they may not always want to die. When you're feeling down, it's easy to focus on the negative and disturbing aspects of your life. This can make suicide seem like the only option. However, there are many reasons to keep living, even when things are tough.

For example, many people have relationships with loved ones, pets they love, religious beliefs, goals and ambitions, or a sense of duty to others. These reasons can help you to stay grounded and prevent you from acting on your suicidal thoughts. When you're feeling down, remind yourself of these reasons.

Coping with suicidal thoughts

Even though it feels like your pain will never end, thoughts about dying are often caused by a mental health problem that can be treated. Depression requires professional intervention. It changes the brain chemistry and affects your feelings, thoughts, and emotions. It can make it difficult or impossible to feel happy, remember positive memories, or come up with solutions to your problems.

If you have been struggling with these thoughts, know that you are not alone. Many people consider suicide for a variety of reasons. Suicidal thoughts can be terrifying. You likely feel hurt, confused, overwhelmed, and hopeless about your future. You may be experiencing sadness, grief, shame, guilt, or emptiness. You may believe that there is nothing you can do to improve your circumstances. Your feelings may seem too much to bear right now. It is important to understand that thinking about ending your life does not mean that you will lose control or act on your thoughts. It does not mean that you are weak or crazy. Many people consider suicide as a way to escape the pain that they are experiencing. There are ways to cope when such thoughts arise.

Identify things that have worked in the past

Think about some things that have helped you feel better in the past when you have faced similar challenges. Here are some examples:

- Having faith and trusting that time will always help
- Reaching out to friends and family
- Seeing a professional
- Attending a support group
- Following a safety plan
- Doing something you enjoy
- Not being alone
- Maintaining a journal
- Not drinking or using drugs

It is important to find out what works best for you and to build a support system around you. If you are struggling, please reach out for help. There are people who care about you and want to help you get through this.

Talk to a trusted one or a mental health professional

Sharing what you are going through with someone you trust is important. Sometimes, just sharing your feelings can help. It is also essential that you are honest about all your emotions. If you have a suicide plan, tell someone about it. People often feel relieved after sharing their feelings with someone. Talking can help you feel less alone and cope with thoughts about ending your life. Ultimately, everyone wants to be heard and validated.

Receive treatment for depression

If you are suffering from depression, anxiety, or substance abuse, it is important to seek therapy. Seeing your primary care physician may not be enough. Visiting a mental health professional, such as a psychologist or a psychiatrist, can be beneficial. You can ask for referrals from your doctor or call a distress helpline number. If you are already receiving therapy, let your therapist know if your treatment plan is not working.

Do the opposite of how you feel

When you experience suicidal thoughts, doing the opposite of how you feel can be helpful. For example, people who are depressed often feel like they want to be alone. However, doing the opposite, such as connecting with others, can alleviate depressive symptoms.

Choosing your words and actions carefully

Depression is a formal mental health diagnosis. It is not something that can be turned on and off at will. Depression has nothing to do with willpower or determination to feel better. This is why it might not go away with a few encouraging words or a motivational pep talk. However, support and compassion can be helpful. And this is where what you say and do can make a big difference. If someone you care about suffers from depression, everything you say can be interpreted differently based on the challenges they are going through. Therefore, you should *avoid* telling them the following:

"Everyone is going through something."

Beyond a traumatic life event, there are multiple causes of depression. Although researchers are still unable to pinpoint the actual cause of the condition, they have identified a few contributing factors, such as chemical imbalances in the brain, side effects of medication, unresolved grief, trauma, abuse, etc. Depression is more than just being sad. It significantly affects a person's capacity to function and interact in life. Even though everyone faces difficulties in life, living with depression is not the same as dealing with problems or having a stressful day. Telling someone to "get over it" invalidates their experiences and concerns. This statement demonstrates a lack of empathy and understanding of what a depression diagnosis entails.

"You just need a drink."

If you have never had depression, it is natural to imagine it as a string of unpleasant days. The media often portrays it this way. However, depression is not about wanting to have a good time or forgetting what you are going through by drinking. Inviting someone with depression to an enjoyable activity may help them in the present, even if it will not cure depression. However, inviting them to consume mainly alcohol may not be advisable. Here is why:

- Alcohol can provide brief emotional and physical relief for some people suffering from depression. But, alcohol is ultimately a depressant and it will make their condition worse.
- People with depression are more likely to turn to alcohol as a coping mechanism, as they may also be experiencing low self-esteem and insomnia.
- People with depression are more likely to develop a substance dependency.

Therefore, it is important to be mindful of the risks of inviting someone with depression to consume alcohol. If you are concerned about their drinking, it is best to talk to them about it. You can also offer to help them find other ways to cope with their depression.

"This too shall pass."

Maybe. But when you're depressed, it doesn't feel like it is going away. When someone is struggling with a mental disorder, it can be difficult to see the light at the end of the tunnel. Depression can feel unrelenting and never-ending. People who are depressed may lose hope when they try to feel better every day, but no relief comes. Telling someone that their sadness will pass can minimize their pain and make them feel unheard. It can also make them feel like you don't understand what they are going through. Instead, assure them that you will be there for them no matter how long they are in pain. You can have a more significant impact than you realize by making someone feel less alone.

"You don't look depressed."

Depression can manifest in many different ways. While it is true that some people with severe depression may stop caring for themselves physically, it is also true that people with depression can appear perfectly healthy. Depression can have different effects on different people. Some people with depression may appear to function normally. They may look after themselves, go to work, and even smile or laugh. However, this does not mean that they are not suffering from internal sorrow and pain.

Are you living a depressive lifestyle?

Depression can be manipulative. It can make us do things that make our depressed mood worse, even though it feels like the right thing to do. When we are depressed, we tend to avoid unpleasant thoughts, feelings, and events. The problem is that these often make us feel worse. So, let's look at what kind of lifestyle choices can trigger or worsen our depression. How many of these activities are you currently engaging in? [Tick mark the ones that apply.]

Don't brush my teeth regularly	Smoke cigarettes	Don't exercise regularly	Skip meals
Eat a lot of junk food	Spend hours on social media	Play video games for hours	Stay indoors all the time
Watch a lot of TV	Don't wash my hair regularly	Don't smile and laugh enough	Sleep all day

Leave tasks unfinished	Think only negative thoughts	Stopped praying or visiting religious places	Physically harm myself
Argue with others	Stay in bed most of the time	Stopped bathing regularly	Stopped seeking help
Listen to mostly sad or angry music	Don't attend meetings regularly	Go to bed at different times of the night	Stopped pursuing my hobbies
Skip classes	Use illegal drugs	Complain a lot	Overeat
Binge drink	Avoid family and friends	Don't organize my room	Get up at different times every morning

You have the power to make changes that support your well-being. Don't be afraid to experiment, find what empowers you, and celebrate your progress, no matter how small. By taking charge of your lifestyle choices, you're actively managing your wellbeing and paving the way for a brighter future.

Putting it all into action

Consider the following prompts to help you reflect on negative thoughts and reframe them in a more positive light.

Check-in with yourself

1. What is something that made you feel sad today? Are you grieving someone or something?

   _____

   _____

   _____

2. What are your negative thoughts at this moment? What are 3 positive thoughts for each of those negative thoughts?

   _____

   _____

   _____

3. What did you do to feel better? What coping mechanisms did you use?

   _____

   _____

   _____

4. Where in your body do you feel the emotional symptoms of depression?

   _____

_____

_____

5. What is making you feel hopeless, and why?

_____

_____

_____

Reflect

1. Looking back, what were some early signs that your emotional wellbeing wasn't at its best?

_____

_____

_____

2. What things or events activate or worsen your low mood?

_____

_____

_____

3. If depression is a messenger, what do you think it is trying to tell you?

_____

_____

_____

4. Is your bedtime routine harmful or helpful to you? How?

_____

_____

_____

5. When you feel hopeless, how do you respond?

_____

_____

_____

Make a change

1. What is one thing you could do that could change your life? What do you need more of in your life?

_____

_____

_____

2. What do you need less of in your life? How could you take steps towards that?

_____

_____

_____

3. What do you feel are the happiness activators in your life? (Things that make you feel happy.)

_____

_____

_____

4. What are your goals for today?

_____

_____

_____

5. What is something you can look forward to?

_____

_____

_____

5

When feelings get physical

How your emotions might be making you ache

It is true that our thoughts and beliefs can create illness in our bodies. Our bodies are always communicating with us, and we can learn a lot about ourselves by paying attention to our physical symptoms. Our thoughts and words have a powerful effect on our cells, and our bodies will eventually reflect our thinking patterns. We must be mindful of our thoughts and words to create a healthy body and mind. In the past, doctors believed that the body and mind were separate entities. However, we now know that the two are closely connected. Stress can have a significant impact on our physical health and can contribute to a variety of conditions. When our bodies experience stress, hormones like cortisol are released. Cortisol has been linked to several physiological changes, including increases in blood pressure, heart rate, and blood sugar levels. These changes can, in turn, weaken the immune system, making us more susceptible to illness. Our thoughts, emotions, and beliefs also play a role in our physical health. Our chemistry and biology influence our moods, emotions, thoughts, and beliefs. When all of these elements are considered together, they can significantly affect our stress and physical health.

While it is true that some ailments, such as a broken bone, are entirely physical, other conditions are not so clear. We know that some medical diseases, especially those that may fall under *chronic* conditions, are often strongly tied to stress. Gastrointestinal disorders, sleep problems, high blood pressure, and long-term pain are just a few examples of diseases caused by or aggravated by high levels of untreated stress. So how does this work? Our thoughts have a powerful effect on our bodies. Negative emotions such as stress, anger, fear, hurt, mistrust, jealousy, and guilt can manifest as disease. Our thoughts and emotions are not separate from our physical bodies. They are all part of the same system. When we experience negative emotions, our bodies release hormone and chemicals that can damage our health. These hormones and chemicals can weaken our immune system, make us more likely to get sick, and worsen existing conditions. Chronic stress can also damage our DNA, which can lead to disease later in life. There is a growing body of research that supports the connection between stress and disease.

On the other hand, positive emotions, such as love, peace, harmony, forgiveness, acceptance, appreciation, trust, and enthusiasm, can have a positive impact on our health. It is important to be aware of our thoughts and how they affect our bodies. When we feel negative emotions, we can focus on positive thoughts instead. This can help to reduce stress, improve our mood, and boost our health. We can clear emotional blockages by forgiving those who have hurt us and releasing resentment. Forgiveness does not mean that we are saying what happened was okay. It simply means that we are choosing to let go of the pain and anger that we are holding onto. When we forgive, we are free to move on with our lives. We can improve our health and well-being by choosing positive thoughts and forgiving those who have hurt us.

Understanding the world through vibration

The body and mind are closely connected. The body is a physical manifestation of the mind, and the mind can influence the body in many ways. For example, if you have a toothache, your mind may be unable to focus on anything else. You may feel agitated, disturbed, and irritated. When the mind is depressed, the body is also affected. This can lead to several physical problems, such as fatigue, pain, and changes in appetite and sleep patterns.

When the mind is healthy, the body is more likely to be healthy as well. This is because the mind and body are constantly communicating with each other. When the mind is positive and relaxed, it releases hormones that promote health and well-being. Our thoughts, emotions, and words create powerful vibrations that resonate throughout our entire body at the cellular level and leave a lasting impression. You can live a happy, harmonious, and peaceful life by replacing negative thoughts with positive ones. For example, if you feel hatred, try to replace that thought with love. If you are feeling fear, try to replace that thought with courage. The thoughts you think will eventually manifest themselves in your actions, habits, character, and destiny. So, it is crucial to be mindful of your thoughts. Choose to think positive thoughts that will lead to a positive life. Human beings create their destiny through their thoughts and actions. They can change the quality of their life by thinking and acting differently. There is no doubt that humans are the masters of their destiny. People can create a better future for themselves by thinking and acting positively.

Every change of thought creates a vibration in the mental body. This vibration is transmitted to the physical body, where it causes activity in the brain. This activity causes electrical and chemical changes in the brain cells. These changes are caused by thought activity. Chronic experiences of intense negative emotions, such as anger, anxiety, and jealousy, may be linked to an increased risk of developing certain health problems, including heart disease, liver disease, and digestive issues. The exact nature of this association is still being researched. It is important to remember that every thought we think impacts our bodies. When we think negative thoughts, we send our cells a message that they are not safe and need to defend themselves. This can release stress hormones, damaging the cells and weakening the immune system. Over time, the adverse effects of negative thoughts can pile up and lead to serious health problems. When we focus our minds on a particular thought, it creates a vibration in the body. The more we focus on that thought, the stronger the vibration becomes. This vibration can eventually become a habit, and we may find ourselves automatically thinking about that thought even when we don't want to. The body is constantly changing in response to our thoughts. For example, our heart rate and breathing may increase if we are feeling anxious. If we feel happy, our muscles may relax, and our faces may light up. The body with its organs is no other than the thought. Violent outbursts of anger may change brain function, impacting memory, decision-making, and even emotional regulation. The mind gets heavily disturbed when we are angry. When the mind is disturbed, the body also gets disturbed. The whole nervous system gets agitated. Anger must be controlled with love. As we think, we vibrate. As we vibrate, we attract. What we think about creates our reality. If we think positive thoughts, we will invite positive experiences into our lives. We can choose to think positive thoughts and create a positive reality for ourselves. We can also choose to focus on the good things in our lives and appreciate what we have. When we do this, we send a message to our bodies that we are safe and happy. This can help to improve our health and well-being.

Exploring the mind-body connection and physical ailments

The mind and body are interconnected, and our thoughts can have a significant impact on our physical health. This information explores the interesting connection between our emotions and physical health. It's important to remember that this is just one piece of the puzzle. If you're experiencing any health problems, always see a doctor to get a proper diagnosis and treatment. However, some people find that considering their emotions alongside physical symptoms can be beneficial. Thinking about how you're feeling might help you take steps towards better overall health. Here are some possible thought patterns that could manifest as a disease in particular body parts:

The head

The head, housing our brain and serving as the window to the world, often becomes the battleground for this mind-body connection. While the exact mechanisms are still being unraveled, research suggests a fascinating interplay between emotions and head-related ailments like headaches and migraines. Stress is a major player in head-related discomfort, and the hormones it releases can constrict blood vessels, leading to tension headaches. Additionally, chronic stress can disrupt sleep patterns, another potential trigger for headaches. Some believe specific emotions can act as triggers for headaches. Anger, frustration, and anxiety might lower our pain tolerance and exacerbate existing tension. The exact cause-and-effect relationship remains under investigation, but some people report experiencing headaches more frequently during periods of emotional turmoil. Migraines, more intense than headaches, can also have an emotional component. Similar to stress, emotional upheavals like anxiety or frustration can trigger a migraine attack. Interestingly, some women experience migraines linked to hormonal fluctuations during their menstrual cycle. If you experience frequent headaches or migraines, it might be beneficial to explore the emotional aspects alongside seeking medical advice. Keeping a headache journal can help identify potential emotional triggers. Techniques like mindfulness and meditation can equip you with tools to manage stress and potentially reduce the frequency and intensity of headaches.

The neck and the throat

The neck and the throat are important parts of our body that allow us to communicate, express ourselves, and create. When we have problems in these areas, it can be a sign of underlying emotional issues. The neck is the bridge between the head and the body, and it represents our ability to see the other side of a situation. Some people believe that neck problems are linked with being inflexible in our thinking. We may be holding on to a rigid point of view, and we are not willing to see things from another perspective. The throat is the gateway to our voice, and it represents our ability to communicate effectively, express ourselves honestly, and stand up for our beliefs. When we have throat problems, it can be a sign that we are feeling silenced or unheard. We may feel inadequate or afraid to speak our truth, and we may be suppressing our voice. The throat also represents our creative flow. Some theories suggest a connection between being creatively stifled and throat discomfort. This is because the throat is the channel through which we express our creativity. When we are not able to express ourselves creatively, we may feel blocked or constricted. The throat chakra, the fifth energy center in the body, is associated with change. When we resist change or are in the midst of it, we may experience physical or emotional symptoms in the throat area. Coughing can be a sign of resistance to change. When you cough, notice what has just been said or done to identify your reaction. Here are some tips for addressing the emotional issue that may be causing neck or throat problems:

- Become aware of your thoughts and feelings. Pay attention to the thoughts and feelings that you have when you are experiencing neck or throat problems. What are you thinking and feeling? Are you feeling angry, frustrated, or afraid?

- Express yourself. Find a safe and healthy way to express your thoughts and feelings. This could be through journaling, talking to a therapist, or creative expression.
- Be open to change. Accept that change is a part of life and that it is not always a bad thing. Embrace change and see it as an opportunity for growth.
- Be creative. Find ways to express your creativity. This could be through art, music, writing, or any other activity that allows you to express yourself freely.

The back

The back is a crucial part of our body, literally supporting us through life's challenges. Some believe that back pain might be linked to our emotional state. The upper back, connecting our heart and mind, could be a reflection of our need for emotional support. Discomfort in this area might be associated with feeling a lack of support from loved ones or colleagues. If you experience upper back pain and suspect it might be linked to emotional needs, consider reaching out to someone you trust. Talking can help you feel supported and navigate challenging situations. The middle back is often seen as a protective shield. Some believe that pain in this area might be associated with feelings of guilt or burdens we carry. If you experience middle back pain and suspect it might be linked to guilt, consider the possibility of forgiveness. Forgiving yourself or others can be a powerful tool for letting go of burdens and promoting emotional well-being. Here are some tips for addressing the emotional issues that may be causing back pain:

- Become aware of your thoughts and feelings. Pay attention to the thoughts and feelings that you have when you are experiencing back pain. What are you thinking and feeling? Are you feeling unsupported, unloved, or guilty?

- Express yourself. Find a safe and healthy way to express your thoughts and feelings. This could be through journaling, talking to a therapist, or creative expression.
- Seek support. Reach out to people who you trust and who can support you. This could be friends, family, therapist, or a support group.
- Forgive yourself. If you are feeling guilty about something, forgive yourself and move on. Holding onto guilt will only make your back pain worse.

The heart

The heart is a symbol of our emotional state. It is the wellspring of joy, and the blood is its messenger. Our hearts pump joy throughout our bodies, nourishing us and keeping us alive. Imagine the heart as a maestro, conducting a symphony within us. When joy infuses our lives, the heart's rhythm becomes a vibrant allegro, potentially contributing to a healthy circulatory system. However, when negativity takes hold, the music might falter, perhaps impacting overall well-being.

This doesn't imply a direct cause-and-effect relationship, but rather a complex interplay. While some research suggests emotional well-being might influence heart health, it's crucial to acknowledge the role of various factors.

The key, perhaps, lies in cultivating a sense of appreciation. Savoring the warmth of the sun on your face, the laughter of loved ones, or the satisfaction of a completed task - these seemingly simple joys might contribute to a more positive emotional state. Such a state might, in turn, be associated with improved cardiovascular health.

The heart is a symbol of love and compassion. It is the place where we feel our emotions most deeply. When we are in love, our hearts open up and we feel connected to them. Where is your heart? Are you someone who is always looking for joy in life, or are you someone who is constantly bogged down by drama? If you want to live a long and healthy life, it is vital to find joy in the simple things and to appreciate the people who love you. Here are some tips for finding joy in life:

- Spend time with loved ones. Our relationships are one of the most important sources of joy in life. Make time for the people who matter to you and let them know how much you care.
- Do things that make you happy. What are the things that make you feel alive? Make time for these activities, even if it's just for a few minutes each day.
- Be grateful. Take some time each day to appreciate the good things in your life. This could be anything from your health and family to your home and job.
- Take care of yourself. Make sure you're getting enough sleep, eating healthy foods, and exercising regularly. When you take care of yourself, you're better able to cope with stress and enjoy life.

The stomach

The stomach is like a gatekeeper, guarding our inner selves from new experiences and ideas. When we have stomach problems, it can be a sign that we are afraid of something new. We may be afraid of not being good enough, of being judged, or of being rejected. This fear can cause us to feel nauseous, bloated, or even to have ulcers. Ulcers are often thought to be caused by a tremendous fear of not being good enough. This fear can be rooted in our childhood, when we may have felt like we were never good enough for our parents, our teachers, or our peers. As adults, this fear can manifest itself in our stomachs, as we try to please others by ripping our guts apart. If we are experiencing stomach problems, it is important to ask ourselves what we are scared of. What new experience or idea are we struggling to assimilate? Once we identify the fear, we can start to confront it and overcome it. Here are some tips for overcoming the fear of new experiences:

- Expose yourself to new things gradually. Don't try to do too much too soon. Start by exposing yourself to small, manageable challenges. As you get more comfortable, you can gradually increase the challenge level.
- Talk to someone you trust about your fears. Talking to someone you trust can help you to feel less alone and more supported. They may also be able to offer you helpful advice.
- Practice relaxation techniques. Relaxation techniques, such as deep breathing and meditation, can help to calm your body and mind. This can make it easier to face your fears.
- Reward yourself for taking risks. When you take a risk and it goes well, reward yourself. This will help you to associate taking risks with positive experiences.

The colon

The colon is like a gate, keeping the past from blocking our path to the future. When we have constipation, it can be a sign that we are holding on to something that we no longer need. This could be anything from old relationships to negative thoughts and emotions. Just like waste that is not eliminated from the body can cause pain and discomfort, holding on to the past can also cause us pain and discomfort. It can prevent us from moving forward in our lives and from experiencing all that life has to offer. If we want to live a full and happy life, we need to learn to let go of the past. This doesn't mean that we have to forget the past or pretend that it never happened. It simply means that we need to accept the past for what it was and release it so that we can move on. We can do this by:

- Forgiving ourselves and others. Holding on to anger and resentment will only keep us stuck in the past. When we forgive ourselves and others, we free ourselves up to move on with our lives.
- Practicing mindfulness. Mindfulness is the practice of paying attention to the present moment without judgment. When we practice mindfulness, we become more aware of our thoughts and emotions. This allows us to see them for what they are and to let them go.
- Focusing on the present moment. The past is gone and the future is not here yet. The only thing that is real is the present moment. When we focus on the present moment, we are able to live our lives to the fullest.

The skin

Our skin is like a cloak that protects our individuality from the world. When we have skin problems, it can be a sign that we feel our identity and individuality are being threatened. We may feel like we are being judged, criticized, or rejected. This can cause us to feel insecure, vulnerable, and exposed. Just like a cloak can be torn or damaged, our skin can also be damaged by the harsh words of others, the critical thoughts of our own minds, or the negative experiences of our past. When this happens, we may feel like we are being skinned alive, and our nerves are right under our skin. One of the quickest ways to heal skin problems is to nurture ourselves by saying in our minds that we approve of ourselves. This means accepting ourselves for who we are, flaws and all. It means letting go of the need to be perfect and the fear of being judged. When we learn to love and accept ourselves, we take back our power. We no longer give others the power to define us or make us feel insecure. We become our own authority, and our skin becomes a symbol of our strength and resilience. Here are some additional tips for healing skin problems from an emotional perspective:

- Identify the negative thoughts and beliefs that are contributing to your skin problems. Once you identify these thoughts and beliefs, you can start to challenge them and replace them with more positive ones.
- Practice self-compassion. When you make a mistake or feel insecure, be kind to yourself. Don't beat yourself up or criticize yourself. Instead, offer yourself understanding and support.
- Take care of your physical health. Eating a healthy diet, getting enough sleep, and exercising regularly can all help to improve your skin health.
- Spend time in nature. Being in nature can help to reduce stress and anxiety, which can contribute to skin problems.
- Connect with loved ones. Strong social support can help to buffer the effects of stress and improve your overall well-being.

The lungs

Our lungs are like a gateway, allowing us to take in life and give it back out. When we have lung problems, it can be a sign that we are afraid to take in life. We may feel like we are not worthy of living fully, or we may be afraid of what life will bring. Just like a gateway can be blocked or closed, our lungs can also be blocked by fear, anxiety, or stress. When this happens, we may find it difficult to breathe, and we may feel like we are suffocating. If we are struggling with lung problems, it is important to ask ourselves why we are afraid to take in life. What are we afraid of? Once we know what we are fearful of, we can work on overcoming our fear. The best way to overcome a fear is to face it head-on. This doesn't mean that you have to do something that you are absolutely terrified of, but it does mean that you should start small and gradually work your way up to bigger challenges. Talking to someone you trust about your fears can help you to feel less alone and more supported. They may also be able to offer you helpful advice.

Stiffness

Stiffness in the body can be like a cage, trapping us in our old ways of thinking. When we are afraid, we may become rigid and inflexible, both physically and mentally. This can lead to stiffness in our bodies as we become less willing to move and explore. Just like a cage can be difficult to break out of, stiffness in the body can be difficult to overcome. However, it is possible to release the stiffness and free ourselves from our old ways of thinking. The first step is to pay attention to where the stiffness is located. This can give us clues about where we are being stiff and rigid in our minds. For example, if we have stiffness in our neck, it may be a sign that we are resisting change. If we have stiffness in our shoulders, it may be a sign that we are carrying too much stress. Once we have identified the areas of stiffness in our body, we can begin to work on releasing them. We can do this through stretching, yoga, or other forms of bodywork. We can also work on releasing the stiffness in our minds by practicing mindfulness and meditation. As we release the stiffness in our bodies and minds, we will find that we become more relaxed and freer. We will be more open to new possibilities and more willing to explore. We will be able to move more easily and fluidly through life.

Identifying negative energy

Apart from manifesting as a disease in the body, negative or low vibrational energy can also show up in the following signs:

We become critical

When we are critical of others, we are essentially saying that they are wrong and we are right. This can make us feel good about ourselves because it gives us a sense of superiority. However, this feeling is often short-lived. We feel empty and insecure once the initial rush of endorphins wears off. This is because we still need to address the root of our insecurity. We have pushed it away by criticizing someone else.

We complain a lot

Complaining is a way of expressing our negative emotions, but it can also be a way of attracting more negativity into our lives. When we complain, we are essentially putting our negative energy out there and inviting others to join in. We are asking them to agree with us and join us in our negativity. This creates a negative feedback loop, where we each feed off each other's negativity.

We can't sleep

When we can't sleep, it can be a sign that we are carrying a lot of negative energy. When we are sleep-deprived, our brains are more likely to focus on negative thoughts. This is because sleep deprivation hampers our ability to regulate our emotions. As a result, we may find ourselves ruminating on negative thoughts, making it difficult to fall asleep or stay asleep. On the other hand, when we are already stressed or anxious, it can be challenging to fall asleep. This is because our bodies are in a state of *fight or flight,* which is not conducive to sleep. As a result, we may find ourselves tossing and turning, unable to relax.

Raise your vibration

We feel positive emotions such as happiness, lightness, and peace when we are in a high vibration. When we are in a state of low vibration, we feel negative emotions such as sadness, heaviness, and confusion. Here's how we can raise our vibrations for an improved state of health:

Meditation

When you train yourself to be present in the moment, you are more in tune with reality. The past and the future are only thoughts; the only truth is the present moment. Meditation and mindful breathing can calm your nervous system, improve your mood, and bring you greater peace – all high-vibration qualities that will benefit your well-being. This spiritual practice can help you raise your vibration quickly and enjoy the benefits immediately.

Gratitude

Gratitude is a powerful emotion that can have a significant impact on our overall well-being. When we are grateful for the good things in our lives, it raises our vibration and attracts more positive experiences into our lives. There are many ways to practice gratitude. One simple way is to take a few minutes each day to think about all the things you are thankful for. You can also write down your blessings in a journal, or create a gratitude jar where you put slips of paper with your gratitude written on them.

Love

Love is one of the highest vibrating states of being. It is a powerful emotion that can have a profound impact on our lives. When we feel love, it raises our vibration and attracts more positive experiences into our lives. One way to experience the power of love is to imagine someone who is easy for you to love. Hold them in your heart and visualize them sitting in front of you. Notice how you feel. You may feel a sense of expansion, lightness, and happiness. This is the shift you are looking for. Love is not just about romantic relationships. It is also about the love we feel for our family, friends, pets, and even strangers. When we open our hearts to love, we become more connected to the world around us and more aware of the good that exists.

Generosity

Generosity is the act of giving without expecting anything in return. It is a powerful emotion that can have a profound impact on our lives. When we are generous, we open ourselves up to the flow of abundance and prosperity. We also create a sense of happiness, peace, and contentment in our lives. When you are stingy or greedy, you are closing yourself off from the flow of abundance. There are many ways to be generous. We can give our time, money, or possessions to others. We can also be generous with our words, our smiles, and our compliments.

Eliminate toxins from your body

Alcohol is a depressant that can temporarily make you feel good. However, it can also lower your vibration and make it harder to live a clear, spiritually connected, and healthy life. If you want to improve your overall well-being, it is important to eliminate toxins from your body. One way to do this is to reduce or eliminate alcohol consumption.

Think positive thoughts

Your thoughts have a powerful impact on your reality. When you think negative thoughts, you are more likely to experience negative events. Conversely, when you think positive thoughts, you are more likely to experience positive events. It is important to remember that your thoughts are not accurate representations of reality. They are simply your interpretation of reality. When you have a negative thought, take a moment to challenge it. Ask yourself if there is any evidence to support the thought. If not, replace the thought with a more positive one. This may not seem easy, but it is a skill that can be learned with practice.

Consume high-vibration music, TV, books, and music

Be mindful of the information you consume and choose things that uplift you rather than deplete you. Consider how different types of media make you feel. Does social media make you energized or insecure? Does watching a violent action film make you feel more anxious or excited? You may be surprised at how much a change in your media intake can improve your day. Choose music that makes you feel good. Watch TV shows and movies that are uplifting and positive. Read books that are inspiring and thought-provoking. Listen to podcasts that are educational and entertaining.

Surround yourself with beauty

Make sure your home and work environments are beautiful, inspiring, and energizing. The right lighting, art, colors, and organization can have a huge impact on your productivity, mood, and overall well-being. Choose light fixtures that create a warm and inviting atmosphere. Avoid harsh fluorescent lighting, which can be tiring and depressing. Instead, choose soft, diffused lighting that will make your space feel cozy and inviting. Decorate with art that you love. Art can be a powerful source of inspiration and beauty. Choose art that speaks to you and makes you feel happy and peaceful. Use colors that make you feel good. Colors can have a big impact on our mood and energy level. Choose colors that you find calming and energizing. Keep your space organized and clutter-free. Clutter can be overwhelming and stressful. Take some time each day to declutter your space and create a sense of order.

Tune in to your feelings

It is often easier to feel physical pain than emotional pain. Physical pain is more straightforward to understand and treat than emotional pain. It is also easier to talk about with others. However, emotional pain can be as natural and debilitating as physical pain.

Consider this example: Jenny had a very intense therapy session in which she felt emotions she did not want to feel from her childhood. She felt ashamed, angry, and hurt. Not long after this session, she developed a strange pain in her right lower back. She imagined many terrible things, like a tumor or a pulled muscle, and consulted a doctor. The doctor did not find anything physically wrong with Jenny, but he suggested that her pain might be caused by emotional stress. He recommended that she see a therapist to help her process her emotions and deal with the pain.

As Jenny thought more about it, she realized that the pain in her back was a way of avoiding the emotional pain that she was feeling. She was using the physical pain to distract herself from the emotional pain. The more she avoided the emotional pain, the worse the physical pain became. It wasn't until she finally faced the emotional pain that the physical pain started to subside. Emotional pain is often difficult to deal with, so it's understandable that Jenny would try to avoid it. However, avoiding emotional pain only makes it worse in the long run. The only way to truly heal from emotional pain is to acknowledge it and face it head-on. Healthy ways to cope with emotional pain include exercise, journaling, and spending time with loved ones. Remember that you are not alone. Everyone experiences emotional pain at some point in their lives.

Our feelings are a valuable source of information. They can guide us, help us understand ourselves, and connect us to the world around us. When we ignore our feelings, they may manifest in unhealthy ways, such as depression, muscle tension, eating disorders, etc. It is important to acknowledge our feelings, feel them, and let them go.

Here is one way to do that.

- Notice a painful or tense area of your body.
- See if it is associated with a thought or feeling.
- Feel the feeling. Instead of trying to suppress the feeling, breathe in and allow yourself to feel it fully.
- Then, exhale and let it go. Repeat this process a few times and see what happens.

It is important to be patient and kind to yourself as you do this. It may take some time to get used to feeling your emotions. But it is worth it. When we acknowledge our emotions, feel them, and let them go, we can start to heal.

Using self-talk to manage pain

The things you say to yourself about pain can affect how much pain you feel. Learning how to control your pain instead of allowing it to control you can lead to greater well-being. What you say to yourself about pain can make it worse or better. For example, if you think, "This pain is unbearable," you will feel more pain. However, if you think, "I can handle this pain," you will feel less pain. It is important to remind yourself that you can control your pain. This is the first step to managing your pain.

Here are some examples of positive self-talk that can help you manage your pain:

- I trust my body's ability to cope with this. All is well.
- This pain is temporary and it too shall pass.
- I am strong, and I will get through this.
- I am not alone in this.
- I am grateful for the things I can still do, even though I am in pain.
- I am safe in my body and I am at ease. Everything is working out for me.
- I give myself permission to heal and become pain-free. My pain dissolves with every passing minute. I am healthy.
- I give myself permission to give and receive love. I am vibrant and resilient.

It is important to repeat these positive self-affirmations to yourself regularly, especially when you are feeling pain. You can also write them down and put them in places where you will see them often, such as on your mirror or on your fridge. By using positive self-talk, you can start to change the way you perceive your pain and take control of your experience. This can lead to significant reduction in pain and an improvement in your overall well-being.

It is essential to be aware of the type of self-talk that we engage in, as it can have a significant impact on our mental and physical health. For example, if we are constantly thinking like a victim, we may be more likely to experience depression and anxiety. If we are constantly thinking like a perfectionist, we may be more likely to experience stress and burnout. If we are constantly thinking like a critic, we may be more likely to experience conflict and isolation. And if we are constantly thinking like a worrier, we may be more likely to experience headaches, stomachaches, and other physical symptoms.

- The victim: The victim sees themselves as powerless and helpless. They believe that bad things happen to them because they are unlucky or because other people are out to get them. They often use phrases like "I can't" or "It's not my fault."

- The critic: The critic is constantly judging and criticizing others. They believe that they are better than everyone else and that they have the right to tell others what to do. They often use phrases like "You should" or "You shouldn't."

- The perfectionist: The perfectionist sets unrealistic standards for themselves and is never satisfied with their own performance. They are constantly criticizing themselves and worrying about making mistakes. They often use phrases like "I should" or "I must."

- The worrier: The worrier is constantly worrying about the future. They believe that bad things are going to happen and that they can't control anything. They often use phrases like "What if?" or "I'm afraid."

	What it promotes	Core beliefs
Victim mentality	Depression	No matter what I do, bad things will keep happening.
		I can't change what happens, so trying is pointless.
		I have no control over what happens to me.
Critic mentality	Low self-esteem	I am insignificant and a burden to others.
		Others' behavior is a direct attack on me.
		Let me reject them before they can reject me.
Perfectionist mentality	Chronic stress and burnout	Nothing I do is worthwhile unless it is perfect.
		I can be good enough only if I meet specific standards.
		Others will accept me only if I am perfect.
Worrier personality	Promotes anxiety	If I am anxious about something, it must mean it is a threat or a problem, so I should worry about it.
		I must think through all the possible things that might happen. Otherwise, I won't be prepared.
		If I don't worry about it, it must mean that I don't care.

The good news is that we can change our self-talk. By becoming aware of our negative thoughts and replacing them with positive ones, we can start to improve our mental and physical health.

Examples of positive self-talk

When we are in pain, it can be easy to focus on the negative aspects of our experiences. However, by reframing our thoughts in a positive way, we can start to change the way we feel about our pain. Here are some other examples of positive self-talk that can help you to manage your pain:

1. I am strong and capable of handling this pain.
2. This pain is temporary and I will get through it.
3. How I think about my pain will impact how I feel.
4. My body is healing, and my faith in this treatment won't let me down.

Remember that dwelling on pain, fatigue, stress, depression, anxiety, and worry can intensify pain, whereas a positive attitude, positive self-talk, physical therapy, heat or cold measures, and relaxation can minimize pain.

Journaling prompts for chronic pain

Chronic pain and other chronic conditions can significantly disrupt daily life. While medical treatments are important, alternative pain management methods can also be helpful. Journaling and repeating positive affirmations can help people cope with the emotional toll of chronic pain. Regular journaling can help lower blood pressure, improve lung and liver function, and boost the immune system. When you write about your pain, you can start to identify patterns and triggers that may be contributing to your pain. This information can help you to develop coping strategies to manage your pain. Here are some tips for pain management:

- Find a place where you won't be interrupted.
- Start by writing about your pain. What does it feel like? Where does it hurt? When does it hurt the most?
- Once you understand your pain better, start to identify

patterns and triggers. What seems to make your pain worse? What seems to make it better?

- Once you have identified patterns and triggers, start to develop coping strategies. This could include relaxation, exercise, or spending time with loved ones.
- Journaling should be a process of self-discovery and healing. Don't be afraid to experiment with different techniques and find what works best for you.

Here are five positive affirmations paired with related journaling prompts that can be very helpful for coping with chronic pain:

1.   *Affirmation:* I am in tune with my body and respect its needs.

Journaling Prompt: What are some signs that your body is telling you to slow down or rest? What do you need to do to feel energized again?

_____

_____

_____

_____

2.   *Affirmation:* I use meditation to manage my pain.

Journaling prompt:

- Sit in a comfortable position and close your eyes.
- Take a few deep breaths, inhaling and exhaling slowly and evenly.
- As you breathe in, imagine breathing in a warm, healing light. This light is filling your body and flowing through your veins. As you breathe out, imagine that you are releasing any pain or discomfort.
- Breathe and visualize the light flowing through your body for a few minutes.
- When you are finished, write about how you feel.

_____

_____

_____

_____

3. *Affirmation:* I am kind and compassionate to my body.

Journaling prompt: How do I show kindness and compassion to my body?

---

4. *Affirmation:* I can manage my pain without suffering.

Journaling prompt: How can I learn to manage my pain without suffering?

---

5. *Affirmation:* I can manage my pain with effective coping strategies.

Journaling prompt: How do I cope with high-pain days? What are some new coping strategies that I would like to try?

6

The habit code

From procrastination to progress

Why is it so hard to stick to good habits? Have you ever tried to start a new routine, only to find yourself giving up after a few days or weeks? If so, you are not alone. Forming new habits is hard. It takes time, effort, and consistency.

There are a few reasons why it is so challenging to develop new habits.

- Our brains are wired to prefer the path of least resistance. This means we're more likely to do easy and familiar things, even if they are not good for us. For example, we might be more likely to eat junk food instead of cooking a healthy meal, or we might be more likely to watch TV instead of going for a walk.

- Change can be scary. It's often easier to stay the same, even if we're unhappy with our current situation. This is because change can be unpredictable and uncomfortable. We might not know what to expect, and we might be afraid of failing.

- We often set unrealistic goals. We all have hopes and dreams, and we usually have a general idea of what those are. For example, we might dream of having a healthy body, being respected by our peers, creating important work, having strong relationships with our family and friends, and sharing love with others. These are all admirable goals, and having something to strive for is essential. But it is also important to be realistic about what we can achieve. Setting too challenging goals can lead to disappointment and frustration.

Consider these scenarios:

1. You finally feel motivated to write your book. You spend the entire weekend writing and making a lot of progress. However, when you return to work on Monday, you feel too tired and stressed to continue writing. You end up putting off writing your book until the following weekend, and then the cycle repeats itself.

2. You are inspired by your friend's stories of traveling to new countries. You start to plan your around-the-world trip, but you quickly become overwhelmed by all the details. You don't know where to start, and you begin to feel anxious about the logistics of traveling. Ultimately, you decide to stay home and save money for another time.

In both these situations, you are experiencing a common problem: *motivation without follow-through.* You are motivated to do something, but you don't have the discipline to keep going. We often get caught up in our desires and motivations, and try to solve all of our problems simultaneously. This can lead to frustration and burnout because our dreams often differ from the actions that will get us there. So, how do we balance our desires for change with the need to build sustainable habits?

Have ambitious goals, but break them down into smaller, more manageable steps

If you want to make a fundamental change in your life, you need to start small. Just like the small habits of brushing your teeth or putting on your seatbelt, you can change your life by starting with small, consistent actions. By starting small, you can make lasting changes in your life. This is because small steps can be done automatically without much thought. And as you make these small changes, you will build momentum and confidence, which will help you make even more significant changes in the future. Our brains are wired to learn and repeat behaviors that are rewarded. So, if we want to form new habits, the best way to start is to make tiny changes that are easy to do and that we can reward ourselves for. Instead of thinking of your life goal as a big, audacious thing that you can achieve only when the time is right, start thinking of it in terms of tiny, daily behaviors you can repeat until success becomes inevitable. For example, if you want to start a business, research your industry for 1 hour daily. It's a small change, but it's something you can do that will help you achieve your goal.

Good habits are like plants. If you plant the right seed (a small, achievable behavior) in the right spot (a routine), it will grow without further coaxing (motivation). This metaphor is helpful because it emphasizes the importance of *consistency* and *small steps* when creating habits. Just as a plant needs water and sunlight to thrive, a habit must be repeated regularly to become ingrained. And just like a plant doesn't need to be constantly motivated to grow, a habit does not need to be motivated to stick. The old way to create a habit is to dive in headfirst, which often leads to failure. The new method is to wade in slowly and gradually until the pattern becomes automatic.

Focus on lifestyle, not life change

We often focus on making significant, life-changing transformations, but sometimes the best way to change our lives is to adopt a new lifestyle. This is because life-changing transformations are often challenging to achieve and maintain, whereas new lifestyles are much easier to adopt and stick to. Even small, seemingly insignificant changes can have a big impact over time. For example, losing 50 pounds would be life-changing, but drinking eight glasses of water is a healthy lifestyle that can improve overall well-being. Life goals are important, but daily habits should support them. Life goals give us something to strive for, but they can also be overwhelming if we don't have a plan to achieve them. If you aim to run a marathon, you might set a daily habit of running for 30 minutes. This may seem like a short time, but it will add up over time and eventually help you reach your goal. The key to success is focusing on the small things we can control rather than the big picture. Remember, it's not about being perfect. It's about making progress.

Identity-based habits

Change is difficult, as you know. We all want to be better individuals – stronger, healthier, more creative and competent, better friends and family members. Even if we are genuinely inspired and start doing things better, it's not easy to maintain new habits. It's more likely that we'll be doing the same things next year than quickly creating a new pattern. Why is this the case? Is there anything we can do to make the transition easier?

The key to forming and maintaining long-lasting habits is to first focus on creating a new identity. Our current behaviors mirror our present identity. What we do now reflects the person we believe we are (consciously or unconsciously). To change our behavior for good, we must start believing new things about ourselves. We need to build identity-based habits. This means we must start acting like the person we want to become. For example, if you're going to become a healthy person, you need to start acting like a healthy person. This means eating healthy foods, exercising regularly, and getting enough sleep. It would also help to surround yourself with people who support your healthy lifestyle.

When we set goals, we often focus on the outcome, such as losing weight or getting stronger. However, these goals are centered around something other than our identity. For example, if we say, "I want to lose 10 kg", we are not saying anything about the type of person we want to be. We are simply stating a desired outcome. A more identity-based goal would be to say, "I want to be the type of person who eats healthy and exercises regularly." This specific goal tells us about the person we want to be. When we set identity-based goals, we are more likely to achieve them because we are not just focused on the outcome. We are also focused on becoming the person who can achieve the result.

To understand the concept of change, it is helpful to consider it occurring on three levels:

- Outcomes: The results that we want to achieve. For example, we might want to lose weight, publish a book, or win a championship.

- Processes: The way that we go about achieving our outcomes. For example, we might create a new workout routine, declutter our desks, or develop a meditation practice.

- Identities: Our sense of self. It includes our beliefs, values, and worldview. For example, we might believe we are capable, worthy, and deserving.

The most lasting and transformative change occurs at the identity level. This is because our identity is the foundation for our behavior and habits. When we change our identity, we are more likely to make lasting changes in our behavior and habits. For example, if we want to lose weight, we might set an outcome goal of losing 10 pounds. This is a good start, but it's not enough. We also need to change our old habits and achieve our desired outcomes. This is because our identity is what drives our behavior. If we believe that we are capable and deserving, we are more likely to take action and make the changes necessary to achieve our goals.

Many people start changing their habits by focusing on the desired result they want to achieve. For example, they might say, "I want to run a marathon." This approach is called *outcome-based habits*. The problem with outcome-based habits is that they often focus on the short term. Focusing on the short term makes us more likely to give up when we don't see immediate results. The alternative is to build *identity-based habits*. With this approach, we visualize the person we want to be. Our beliefs about ourselves are powerful drivers of our behavior. If we believe that we are capable and deserving, we are more likely to take action and make the changes necessary to achieve our goals. On the other hand, if we believe that we are not capable or deserving, we are more likely to give up when things get tough.

To form identity-based habits, we need to change our beliefs about ourselves. We need to start believing that we are the type of person who can achieve our goals. We need to believe that we are capable, deserving, and worthy. Here are two steps you can follow to visualize yourself as the person you want to be.

1.

Decide the type of person you want to be. Reflect on the following questions:

What do you want to stand for?

_____

_____

What are your principles and values?

_____

_____

Who do you wish to become?

_____

_____

2.

Prove it to yourself with small wins. Start by taking small steps that align with your desired identity. Celebrate your successes, no matter how small. As you continue to take action, your beliefs will start to change.

Here is an example of how you can make this work in real life:

Want to be a better friend?

Identity: Become the type of person who stays in touch.

Small win: Make an effort to call one friend every Sunday. If you repeat the same people every three months, you will stay close to 12 people throughout the year.

Overcoming obstacles in habit formation

Building habits takes work, and there can be challenges along the way. Other people in your life may resist your efforts. If you start eating healthier, your family members may try to lure you into eating unhealthy foods. Or, if you start exercising more, your friends may make fun of you for working out. Your environment can also make it difficult for you to change your habits. If you live in a busy city, finding time for exercise can be challenging. Or, if you live in a cold climate, it can take a lot of work to get motivated to go outside and walk. Unexpected crises can arise, making sticking to your new habits difficult. If you are sick or have a family emergency, finding the time or energy to exercise or eat healthily can be tricky. It's possible that you'll lose interest in your new habits. This can happen for various reasons, such as the habit becoming too challenging or tedious.

Set up a timer

If you don't feel like reading or meditating, set a timer for 5 minutes and do it anyway. This is a great way to overcome procrastination and get started on the things you know you should be doing. Once you have started reading or meditating, you are more likely to keep going than if you had stopped after 5 minutes. This is because your brain starts to flow, and you become more absorbed in the activity. Committing to doing something for just 5 minutes seems much more manageable than doing it for an hour or more. This can help you overcome the initial inertia and get started. You are also less likely to burn out or get discouraged.

Block time for it

Simple and mechanical habits are easier to form than creative habits. Simple habits, such as reading or meditating, can be done quickly and easily without much planning or effort. However, creative habits, such as creating videos for YouTube, require more time and planning. It is easy to say that you *want* to do something, but it is much harder to make the time for it. Don't create a new video every day if you don't have the time or energy. Start with a smaller goal, such as making one video per week. The most important thing is to start. The most time-consuming and tedious aspects of video creation are not the actual filming and editing. The smaller tasks must be done beforehand, such as getting into the right mindset, preparing the choreography, setting up the lights, and creating the environment. By committing to a specific time slot for your creative habits, you can plan and finish these smaller tasks ahead of time. By doing this, you can focus on the actual creation of the video without worrying about anything else. Just like any other habit, you need to make creating videos a priority. This means scheduling time for it in your calendar and sticking to it. If you don't make it a priority, it will be easy to let it fall by the wayside.

Strengthen your 'why'

Despite our best efforts to stay accountable, it can be difficult to commit to our goals. Tracking habits in a bullet journal or sharing daily updates on social media or with an accountability partner can be helpful, but it's not enough. The reason is that we quickly lose the willpower to keep showing up without revisiting our *whys*.

What are the reasons we want to achieve our goals? What will we gain by doing so? It becomes easy to give up when we lose sight of our *whys*. To avoid this, it is vital to invest some time to read and understand more about the habits we want to develop. We should also keep reminding ourselves of our *whys* regularly. For example, seeing professional athletes train for hours daily can motivate us to work hard at our sport. If we want to be the best we can be, we must put in the same effort. Similarly, students who see their classmates getting good grades are motivated to study harder.

Breaking bad habits

Understanding how habits work can help us break and form good habits. Many of our daily activities are based on habits, such as how we get ready in the morning, the route we take to work, and the groceries we buy on the way home. Habits can be helpful. They provide structure and stability in our lives. However, they can also be harmful if they are negative. For example, if we have a habit of smoking or overeating, it can be challenging to break that habit. This is because of the way our brains work. When we perform a behavior repeatedly, the neurons in our brain that are responsible for that behavior form strong connections. The more we perform the behavior, the stronger those connections become. This is known as *neuroplasticity.* Breaking bad habits can be tricky, even when we know they are bad for us. When you break an unhealthy habit, you are essentially trying to change the wiring of your brain. You need to find new behaviors to replace the old ones, and you need to do this consistently over time.

Habits are formed by the brain creating neural pathways between neurons associated with a particular behavior. The more you perform a behavior, the stronger these neural pathways become. This is why it can be difficult to break bad habits. Breaking a bad habit requires weakening these neural pathways and creating new ones. This can be done by:

- Identifying your triggers. What are the things that make you want to engage in the bad habit? Once you know your triggers, you can start to avoid them or develop strategies for coping with them.
- Finding a replacement behavior. What is something else you can do that will give you the same satisfaction as the bad habit? For example, if you smoke when you're stressed, you could try taking a few deep breaths or going for a walk instead.

Understand the rewards that bad habits bring

Bad habits are often rewarding in some way, even if the reward is short-term or negative. For example, smoking provides a temporary sense of relaxation, while overeating may give a feeling of comfort or satisfaction. Procrastination may provide relief from stress or a feeling of control. Once you understand the rewards your bad habits offer, you can find healthier ways to get those rewards. For example, if you smoke to relax, you could try:

- Exercising: Exercise releases endorphins, which have mood-boosting effects.
- Listening to music: Music can be a great way to relax and de-stress.
- Meditating: Meditation can help you calm your mind and body.

If you overeat to comfort yourself, you could try:

- Journaling: Journaling can help you process your emotions and identify what's causing you to feel stressed or upset.
- Talking to a friend: Talking to a trusted friend or family member can help you feel supported and less alone.
- Practicing self-care: Taking some time for yourself to do something you enjoy can help you relax and de-stress.

Impose a penalty or remove the reward

It is best if you stopped rewarding yourself to break a bad habit. One way to do this is to impose a penalty or take away a desired reward when you relapse. For example, if you overeat, you could give up dessert for the rest of the day or add 10 minutes to your next workout. The penalty or reward should be relevant to the habit. This can be a difficult step, as it requires strong willpower. However, it is important to remember that the more you reward yourself for bad behavior, the more likely you are to continue it. You can break the cycle of rewarding bad habits by imposing a penalty or taking away a desired reward.

Find a replacement

Finding a healthy replacement can help us break habits. For example, if you procrastinate because you enjoy the short-term increase in free time, you could try setting up a more realistic schedule that allows for more regular breaks. You could do something you enjoy during your breaks, such as reading, listening to music, or taking a walk. This way, you can still get the reward of free time, but without the downside of procrastination. Instead of smoking to relieve stress, you could try exercising, meditating, or spending time in nature. If you overeat to comfort yourself, you could try journaling, talking to a friend, or listening to music. If you drink alcohol to socialize, you could try non-alcoholic drinks, such as sparkling water or herbal tea. Finding healthy replacements for your bad habits may take time and effort, but it is worth it.

Use a combination of small and big rewards

Rewards can significantly impact our behavior, and behavioral psychology has shown that rewarding ourselves early and often can help us break bad habits. For example, if you want to break a laziness habit, you might reward yourself with new gym clothes after 30 workouts. However, this reward is so far away that you might need more to motivate you to keep going. Instead, you could break the 30 workouts down into smaller goals, such as working out for 30 minutes 3 times a week. Then, reward yourself with a small treat after each workout. This will ensure you stay motivated and on track to reach your goal. Some examples of small, frequent rewards include:

- Watching your favorite TV show after a workout
- Getting a massage after a long day at work
- Eating your favorite dessert after finishing a project.

Whatever you choose to reward yourself with, it is important to ensure it is something you *want*. This will help you stay motivated and on track to breaking your bad habit. In addition to small, frequent rewards, you can also give yourself big rewards for reaching major milestones. For example, if you want to lose 10 pounds, you could reward yourself with a new outfit after you reach your goal weight. Big rewards can help you stay motivated and on track to achieving your long-term goals.

Let others know about your goals

Shame can be a powerful motivator to achieve our goals. When we tell others about our goals, we are more likely to stick to them because we don't want to disappoint them. However, it's important to tell our goals to people who will support us and not ridicule us if we fail. We set a standard for ourselves when we tell others about our plans. If we don't achieve our goals, we will feel disappointed in ourselves and may also disappoint the people we tell. This can be a powerful motivator to keep us on track. We are essentially making a promise to them. This can make us feel more accountable and less likely to give up. Telling others about our goals also allows us to build a support network. This can be helpful when we feel discouraged or need help staying on track. However, it's important to remember that shame can also be a negative motivator. If we are too focused on avoiding shame, we may become paralyzed by fear and never take risks. It's essential to balance using shame as a motivator and avoiding it altogether. If we consider telling others about our goals, choosing the right people is important. Choose people who will support you and not ridicule you if you fail. You want people who will be there for you, no matter what.

Habits that deplete your mental health

Mental health is an essential part of our overall well-being. However, many people do things that negatively impact their mental health without realizing it. Here are some everyday bad habits that can hurt mental health.

Overusing social media

Social media can be a valuable tool for staying connected with friends and family, but it can also be a source of stress and anxiety. Here are some of the ways that social media can contribute to stress and anxiety:

- Comparison: We often compare our lives to the carefully curated images and stories we see on social media. This can lead to feelings of inadequacy, envy, and depression.
- Fear of missing out (FOMO): We see our friends and family having fun and doing exciting things. This can make us feel like we are missing out, leading to anxiety, loneliness, and social isolation.
- Perfectionism: Social media can create unrealistic expectations about what life should be like. This can lead to feelings of inadequacy and self-doubt.
- Cyberbullying: Social media can be used to bully and harass others. This can lead to feelings of fear, anxiety, and depression.

- Addiction: Social media can be addictive. Spending too much time on social media can lead to problems with focus, productivity, and relationships.

Living a sedentary lifestyle

During the COVID-19 pandemic, many people have been forced to stay home for long periods of time. This has led to a sedentary lifestyle for many people, which can negatively affect mental health. A sedentary lifestyle is one where you spend most of your time sitting or lying down. This can lead to several health problems, including obesity, heart disease, and diabetes. It can also cause mental health problems such as depression, anxiety, and low self-esteem. When we exercise, our bodies release endorphins, which have mood-boosting effects. Endorphins are often called *feel-good chemicals* because they reduce pain and create euphoria. They are released in response to physical activity, so it is recommended that we get off the couch and move every once in a while.

Not sleeping enough

It is okay to stay up late occasionally to watch TV, but don't make it a habit. Sleep is vital for physical and mental health. It allows your body and mind to rest and repair. When you don't get enough sleep, it can affect your mood, energy levels, motivation, and mental health. Sleep deprivation can also lead to depression and anxiety, making sleeping even harder. Here are some of the negative consequences of not getting enough sleep:

- Physical problems: Fatigue, weight gain, and a weakened immune system.
- Cognitive problems: Difficulty focusing, learning, and making decisions.
- Mood problems: Mood swings, anxiety, and depression.

- Behavioral problems: Increased risk of lashing out at others or making poor choices.

Chasing perfectionism

Striving for excellence is good, but it is important to remember that perfection is unattainable. Perfectionism can lead to anxiety, stress, and a fear of failure. It can also prevent you from taking risks and trying new things. Perfectionists often worry about making mistakes and not being good enough. This can lead to anxiety and stress. They are often afraid of failing, which can prevent them from taking risks and trying new things. This can limit their opportunities for growth and learning.

Suppressing feelings

Suppressing emotions can have negative short-term and long-term consequences. Suppressing emotions is the act of refusing to acknowledge or express our feelings. This can lead to a number of negative consequences, both in the short-term and the long-term. In the short-term, suppressing emotions can lead to:

- Anxiety: When we suppress our emotions, they don't go away. They just get pushed down and bottled up. This can lead to anxiety, as our bodies are flooded with stress hormones.
- Depression: Depression is another common consequence of suppressing emotions. When we don't allow ourselves to feel our emotions, we can become overwhelmed and hopeless.
- Physical health problems: Suppressing emotions can also lead to physical health problems, such as stomach aches, headaches, and muscle tension.

In the long-term, suppressing emotions can lead to:

- Substance abuse: People who suppress their emotions are more likely to abuse alcohol and drugs as a way to cope with their feelings.
- Relationship problems: Suppressing emotions can also lead to relationship problems. When we don't communicate our feelings to others, it can lead to misunderstandings and conflict.

Living in a messy environment

Clutter can harm our mental and physical health. It can make us feel anxious, stressed, and, overwhelmed. It can also lead to problems with sleep, decision-making, and productivity. If you are surrounded by clutter, relaxing and enjoying life can be difficult. It can create a sense of chaos and disorder, which can trigger feelings of stress, making it difficult to focus on anything, as your mind constantly tries to process all of the visual information. Falling asleep or staying asleep can also become uncomfortable in a chaotic environment.

Putting your partners' needs before yours all the time

It's important to consider your partner's feelings in a relationship, but it's also important to take care of yourself. Neglecting your needs to please your partner can lead to codependency, an unhealthy relationship where one person gives and gives while the other takes and takes. Here are some signs that you might be in a codependent relationship:

- You feel guilty or selfish when you do something for yourself.
- You find it difficult to say no to your partner.

- You are always putting your partner's needs before your own.
- You feel like you can't live without your partner.
- You are afraid of losing your partner.
- You are constantly trying to please your partner.
- You feel like you are responsible for your partner's happiness.

Failure mindset

Everyone has negative thoughts sometimes, but if we dwell on them, they can become a problem. Negative thoughts like "I am a failure" or "My life is hopeless" can lead to a failure mindset, making it difficult to succeed. These thoughts can keep us up at night and prevent us from taking action during the day. They can become a habit if we don't address them. Thoughts and feelings can have a devastating impact on our mental health. When we fail, it is easy to start thinking negatively about ourselves. We may believe we are not good enough, will never succeed, or are worthless. These negative thoughts can be challenging to overcome, leading to mental health problems, including anxiety, depression, reluctance to set goals, diminishing the value of our natural talents, or magnifying missteps. People with a failure mindset are more likely to have negative self-talk, believe they are incapable of success, and avoid taking risks.

Making excuses

When you blame others, you give up your power to control your destiny. You are saying that you cannot achieve your goals on your own and that you need someone else to change for you to succeed. This is a disempowering mindset that will only hold you back. Instead of blaming others, it is important to take responsibility for your actions and choices. This does not mean that you cannot acknowledge the challenges that you face. It simply means that you should not let these challenges prevent you from acting.

Habits that support mental health

Mental health is a critical component of overall well-being. It is important to take care of mental health just as you would take care of your physical health. The small habits you do everyday shape who you are and the life you live. This can be daunting or liberating, as much of your life is within your control. If you want to create a better life for yourself, it is important to start by focusing on the small habits you can control. How you speak to yourself, how you treat others, how you spend your time, and how you take care of your health add up over time and either improve or degrade the quality of your life.

There are many good mental health habits that you can start practicing today. Incorporating them into your daily life can improve your mental health and well-being. It is important to remember that everyone is different, and what works for one person may not work for another. Experiment with different habits and find what works best for you. And don't be afraid to ask for help when you need it.

Below is a list of 50 mental health positive habits. How many of them do you follow? Tick mark and see for yourself!

Have a few minutes of alone time daily	Make one person smile every day	Devote time to praying	Have a daily look-forward-to list	Declutter your phone
Pay attention to personal grooming	Recite positive affirmations	Learn something new	Practice positive thinking	Declutter your mailbox

Practice gratitude	Limit alcohol	Set work limits	Set boundaries	Listen to podcasts
Pursue hobbies	Journal daily	Make your bed	Volunteer	Meditate
Limit screen time	Stay organized	Hydrate	Get up early	Go to bed early
Mix with new cultures	Practice deep breathing	Get some fresh air	Eat organic and healthy food	Donate to a charity
Eat on a consistent schedule	Say no to what you can't take on	Be mindful of the information you consume	Spend time outdoors	Spend time with successful people
Do some coloring	Socialize	Engage in self-care	Fact-check yourself	Appreciate yourself

Self-reflective questions on maintaining growth and productivity

Self-reflection is the act of thinking about your thoughts, feelings, and experiences. It involves paying attention to your inner world and trying to understand what you are thinking and feeling. Introspection is the act of looking inward to understand your mind and motivations. It involves trying to understand why you think and feel the way you do. When you engage in self-reflection and introspection, you can learn more about yourself, your strengths and weaknesses, and your values. This can help you make better decisions, improve your relationships, and live more fulfilling lives. Self-reflection and introspection are not always easy, but they are worth it. By taking the time to understand yourself better, you can grow, develop your mind, and live a more fulfilling life.

Here are a few questions to ask yourself as you continue on your path of self-development:

1. If this were the last day of my life, would I have the same plans for today?

_____

_____

_____

2. If not now, then when?

_____

_____

_____

3. Why do I matter?

_____

_____

_____

4. What do I want to be remembered for?

_____

_____

_____

5. Who has had the most significant impact on my life?

_____

_____

_____

6. The two moments I will never forget are

_____

_____

_____

7. What words would I like to live by?

_____

_____

_____

8. What would you do if you loved yourself unconditionally?

_____

_____

_____

9. Write the words you need to hear.

_____

_____

_____

10. Write down all things you would like to say yes to.

_____

_____

_____

7

I am enough, and more

From self-criticism to a love story

Many people are familiar with the concept of *self-love,* but they may not fully understand it. Just like we need food to survive, we need self-love to thrive. We often spend our time trying to find love, success, and happiness in the external world, but we often overlook the fact that self-love is the foundation for all of these things. We cannot truly love others without first loving ourselves. When we love ourselves *conditionally*, we are telling ourselves that we are only worthy of love if we meet certain standards. This is a very limiting way of thinking, and it will prevent us from having healthy, fulfilling relationships.

Our understanding of self-love is often developed during childhood. We learn about it from the people who care for us, and we model our behavior after theirs. We see around us many well-groomed people who may not necessarily love themselves. Self-love is more than just wearing nice clothes and makeup. It is about caring for ourselves physically, mentally, emotionally, and spiritually. It is about treating ourselves with the same kindness and compassion as a friend, even when we make mistakes. It is about accepting ourselves for who we are, including our flaws and weaknesses. When we love ourselves, we are better able to love others. We are also better able to cope with stress and adversity. Self-love is the essential foundation for a happy and content life.

Self-love is a concept that comprises four aspects: self-awareness, self-worth, self-esteem, and self-care. When these four aspects are aligned, we can love ourselves unconditionally. However, if one of them is missing, we cannot fully love ourselves. The journey of achieving self-love takes work. It requires us to confront our demons and face our fears. It also requires us to change our lives by letting go of toxic relationships and bad habits.

Self-awareness

Self-awareness is the ability to understand our own thoughts, feelings, and behaviors. It is the awareness of our thought processes, which mainly include our thoughts, how they impact our feelings, and how these feelings cause us to act. Have you ever noticed how your thoughts make you angry and act impulsively? Where do you think these thoughts appeared from, and why are they here? Why do our thoughts make us work the way they do? Why do some ideas make us happy? Self-awareness is all about stepping out of ourselves to examine and analyze ourselves objectively. When we can observe ourselves critically, our emotional intelligence improves. Understanding what irritates us may not stop it, but it will help us know how to respond appropriately. People with high intelligence experience feelings in the same way that we do. The difference is that they are able to step out of their emotions to process them effectively. This includes moving away or avoiding situations that they know will trigger certain undesirable feelings and reactions within them. If we cannot move away or avoid the problem, self-awareness can allow us to redirect our energy to those emotions.

Self-worth

Every day, we are bombarded with negative messages from society. These messages tell us we are not good enough or worthy of love and respect. As a result, we often start to believe these messages and lose our self-worth. The truth is that we are all born with an endless sea of potential. We can do great things to make a difference in the world. We need to believe in ourselves. Self-worth is not determined by anything outside of us. Our looks, possessions, or accomplishments do not define it. *Self-worth is a decision that we make.* It is a decision to believe in ourselves, to value ourselves, and to love ourselves unconditionally. Think about all the good things about yourself. What are you good at? What do you love to do? What do other people appreciate about you? When you focus on the positive, you will feel better about yourself. You will start to believe in yourself. And when you believe in yourself, you can achieve anything you set your mind to.

Self-esteem

Self-esteem is born from self-worth. It is the confidence we have in our abilities and worth. It is the belief that we are valuable and worthy, regardless of our achievements or qualities. Self-worth is often developed in childhood, based on how we were loved and cared for. It can also be influenced by the accomplishments of others in our age group and how we compare to our childhood caregivers. We are more likely to have high self-esteem when we have a strong sense of self-worth. When we have a strong sense of self-worth, we are more likely to be content and comfortable with who we are, where we are, and what we have. We are also more likely to have high self-esteem. Remember, you do not need to justify your experience. You are enough just the way you are.

Self-care

Self-care is the practice of taking actions that promote our physical, mental, and emotional health. It is an essential part of self-love that is not always easy, as it can be challenging to make time for ourselves, especially when we are busy with work or other obligations. However, it is essential to make self-care a priority. When we care for ourselves, we can better care for others and live a happy and fulfilling life. Here is a question you can ask yourself to help you practice self-care: "What would someone who respects and values themselves do?" This question can help you make decisions that are in your best interest, both in the short-term and the long-term. It can also help you to make choices that are in alignment with your values and that will promote your well-being.

For example, if you are feeling stressed, you might ask yourself: "What would someone who respects and values themselves do to reduce stress?" The answer might be to take a break, go for a walk, or listen to some calming music. Or, if you are feeling overwhelmed, you might ask yourself: "What would someone who respects and values themselves do to take care of themselves?" The answer might be to ask for help, delegate tasks, or take a day off. By asking yourself this question, you can start to make choices that are in alignment with your values and that will promote your well-being. This can help you to feel better about yourself and to live a happier and more fulfilling life.

People-pleasing

Are you someone who goes above and beyond to make someone else happy? Do you do things for people hoping they would like you, appreciate you, or not be upset with you?

There is a well-known parable in the Middle East about a father and his son who were traveling to a town on a donkey. While walking, they overheard some people complaining that the boy was riding the donkey while the father was walking. The son felt terrible and asked his father if he could walk instead. The father agreed, but then they overheard other people complaining that the father was making his son walk. The father and son did not know what to do. They did not want to upset anyone, but they did not want to be criticized. In one version of the story, the father and son try to please everyone. They both get on the donkey, but then they overhear someone complaining that they are overburdening the animal. The father and son are so frustrated that they try to pick up the donkey and carry it. But they are not strong enough and end up falling into the river.

The moral of the story is that it is impossible to please everyone. No matter what we do, there will always be someone unhappy. So, we should focus on doing what is best for ourselves and our loved ones without worrying about what others think. While there's nothing wrong with wanting to make others happy, people-pleasing can sometimes lead individuals to their own detriment.

Often misunderstood as simply kind, people who prioritize the needs and desires of others will exhibit the following traits:

Have low self-worth	Accommodate everyone else's needs	Undermine own needs
Are too agreeable in general	Do not assert themselves	Go with the flow that is dictated by others
Rarely say no	Feel valuable when complying with others	Value praise from others
Say sorry when no apology is required	Take the blame, when not at fault	Make excuses for the fault of others

It can be tricky to know the difference between pleasing others and acting out of love. Serving others in love is something we are taught to do, and those who are served frequently enjoy the service.

The main difference between pleasing others and acting out of love is *motive*. What motivates you to do what you do? Do you crave people's approval? Do you yearn to be liked by others? For example, why did you stay up late to finish that project even though you were already sleep-deprived? Did you really do it out of goodwill?

If so, your loss of sleep was worth it. Or was your motive to avoid someone's disappointment? Be truthful. Your response will help you explore your tendencies in relationships.

When we are too polite and kind, we may find ourselves putting the needs of others before our own. We may say yes when we mean no, and we may avoid setting boundaries with demanding or abusive people. This can lead to us feeling resentful, exhausted, and even depressed. Most of us want to belong and build long-lasting relationships with others. And it hurts us a lot when others reject or criticize us. We are afraid of being alone because we believe that being alone indicates that we are inadequate or unlovable. So, we go to great lengths to satisfy people to escape rejection or abandonment.

Have you ever wondered what events shape individuals into people-pleasers? What factors lead to their fear of rejection, abandonment, conflict, or criticism? If you are trying to understand why you might be engaging in people-pleasing tendencies, here are some possible answers:

- Your childhood: If you grew up in a family where you were taught that your worth was based on how much you pleased others, you may have developed a people-pleasing pattern as a way to cope. For example, if your parents were critical or demanding, you may have learned that the only way to avoid their disapproval was to always do what they wanted.
- Your relationships: If you've had relationships with people who were controlling or manipulative, you may have learned to put their needs before your own in order to avoid conflict. For example, if you've been in a relationship with someone who was emotionally abusive, you may have learned that the only way to keep them happy was to always say yes to them, even when it meant sacrificing your own needs.
- Your self-esteem: If you have low self-esteem, you may be more likely to people-please as a way to feel validated

and accepted by others. For example, if you believe that you're not good enough or that you're not worthy of love, you may be more likely to go out of your way to please others in order to earn their approval.

Yes, we should think about others. We should consider their feelings and needs, but we shouldn't only care about them while ignoring or suppressing our own thoughts and needs. You are just as important as others. And yet, many of us act as if we don't matter much, if at all. We are more concerned with others than with ourselves. This may sound like a childhood value, but it is not sustainable. You cannot stay healthy, patient, kind, energetic, and compassionate if you continuously give but never replenish your needs. This takes us to another common issue: we don't believe we should have any needs or act like we don't need anything. We want to be approachable, low-maintenance, and pleasant. Again, agreeableness is desirable, but it is unrealistic to expect your wants, views, interests, and values to always coincide with those of others. We will have disagreements with others from time to time, and that is fine. Healthy partnerships can withstand and resolve differences. Everyone has needs. They could be basic needs such as food, clothing, and shelter, to more complex ones, including the need for belonging, physical affection, mental stimulation, and spiritual enlightenment. When we do not meet our needs, we become physically exhausted and sick, irritable and resentful, disheartened or hopeless. It is important to balance our concern for others with our concern for ourselves. We need to take care of ourselves in order to be able to take care of others. This means meeting our own needs, both physical and emotional. It also means setting boundaries with others so that we do not overextend ourselves. When we take care of ourselves, we are better able to give to others from a place of strength and abundance. We are also more likely to have healthy and fulfilling relationships.

Here are some questions you can ask yourself to start your self-reflection:

What are some of your commonly unmet needs? Do you feel like you need more time for yourself? Do you need more physical touch? Do you need more emotional support?

_____

_____

_____

_____

_____

How do you feel when you don't exercise self-care or voice your thoughts and desires? Do you feel drained, stressed, or resentful? Do you feel like you're not being heard or understood?

_____

_____

_____

_____

_____

Why do you dismiss your own needs and ideas? Do you think your needs are unimportant? Do you think your ideas are not good enough? Do you worry about what others will think if you speak up?

_____

_____

_____

_____

_____

What will happen if you do this? If you continue to dismiss your own needs and ideas, you may become more and more unhappy and unfulfilled. You may also start to resent others and feel like they don't care about you. In the long run, this could lead to health problems, relationship problems, and even depression.

_____

_____

_____

_____

_____

When we consider standing up for ourselves or establishing a boundary, we may have thoughts like:

"Will they be upset?"

"They are going to judge me."

"I'm a bad person."

"They will think I'm being difficult."

These are assumptions, and they can contribute to people-pleasing behaviors. We often have no idea what other people think of us, and our observations are filtered through our beliefs and negative biases. So, it's possible that our assumptions are incorrect. Of course, some people will despise us and our actions. That's unavoidable. We can't control what people think of us, but we can control our own thoughts, feelings, and actions. If we want to stop people-pleasing, we need to start challenging our assumptions about what other people think of us. We can do this by asking ourselves questions like:

- What evidence do I have that other people will be upset if I stand up for myself?
- What is the worst thing that could happen if I establish a boundary?
- What is the most likely outcome if I stand up for myself or establish a boundary?

Once we start to challenge our assumptions, we can start to see that they may not be as true as we thought. We may also start to realize that we are more capable of handling the negative reactions of others than we thought. It's also important to remember that we are not bad people for wanting to stand up for ourselves or establish boundaries. In fact, it is a sign of strength and self-respect. When we take actions that align with our values and make us feel good, we are taking care of ourselves and setting a good example for others.

Coping with feeling lonely

Loneliness is not always caused by isolation. The deepest loneliness comes from a lack of self-esteem. Self-worth, or recognizing your inherent worth, gives you resilience and anchors you. Without it, you are dependent on others to boost your mood.

What is loneliness, exactly? Loneliness is a feeling of isolation. It can be caused by being isolated from other people, but many people feel lonely even though they have family, friends, colleagues, and a large social network. If you can't value and enjoy your own company, only certain relationships can alleviate loneliness. Quality presence is essential in the most fulfilling relationships. They are unmatched. However, if you know you can give yourself genuine attention and self-esteem, you are not quick to seek attention elsewhere. You may still appreciate and value it, but not having attention will not leave you devastatingly lonely. We've all noticed how some people are more present when we're with them than others, and how wonderful that intimacy feels. Giving yourself a high level of presence and respect helps to alleviate the sense of isolation. It relieves loneliness and provides a strong foundation.

If your partner or family members don't accept you for who you are, you may feel lonely. Unsatisfactory relationships have a bigger impact if you rely on them to make you feel special and worthwhile. Feeling unaccepted by others when you don't accept yourself will undoubtedly lead to loneliness. It puts you in an uncomfortable position. It creates a disconnect between your true nature, higher self, and a healthy self-image. Social connectedness is defined as intimacy with another individual. Both connections benefit one's life, but one will always feel lonely without self-esteem. Because your sense of worth is poor and your well-being is dependent on others, you will be upset and emotionally isolated. You are like a sailboat adrift in a storm without constructive input. Allow self-esteem to serve as your anchor. It's not so much about connecting with others as it is about connecting with yourself. Of course, it is human nature to thrive in healthy relationships. But we're mainly talking about loneliness caused by feeling isolated, whether or not you have people around you. It's comforting to know that when you connect with your inner nature, you are less lonely, no matter your circumstances. This is beneficial because it indicates that you can reduce your self-esteem dissatisfaction even if you live alone or don't get along with the people you see most. Connecting with yourself allows you to see things from a different perspective. If your partner doesn't understand you, you can safely rely on your inner resilience because you don't base your self-esteem on their opinion. You identify your inner light and *know* who you are. When you are connected to your essence, someone's disrespectful or disagreeable actions will not harm you.

Checking in with yourself

Constantly moving on autopilot and failing to check in with yourself can have a significant impact on your mental health and ability to stay present. When you're constantly disconnected from the present moment, it can be more difficult to manage stress, process emotions, and pay attention. Imagine working alongside someone with whom you have a great relationship all day, but then you completely avoid them or choose not to check in with them in any way. There would be no casual "Hello, how's it going?" or asking if they have a full afternoon ahead. This scenario sounds a bit odd, right? You would almost certainly initiate some connection at some point, wouldn't you? Going through an entire day without checking in with yourself is similar. It's awkward, and you've missed out on countless opportunities to connect.

You go through many transitions throughout the day. You move from one place to another, from one role to another, and from one task to another. As you go about your day, different emotions and thoughts arise, giving you the choice to engage with them. Some are helpful, while others can lead to self-sabotage. Observing patterns and triggers promotes affirmation and growth rather than avoidance and suppression. Consider these changes as opportunities to pause and reconnect with yourself. Checking in does not mean fully engaging with or analyzing an emotion before moving on. It is simply a scan, a check-in, and a way to connect with yourself and your surroundings. The goals are to collect data and clear your slate. You may not feel any relief, connection, or clarity at first, or you may only feel it for a few seconds. Keep going! This practice takes repetition, so be patient. With each effort, you connect with yourself and identify behavioral and thinking patterns.

What does an effective self-check-in look like?

Pay attention to how you go through your day and how often you transition. Which transitions or tasks happen frequently, if not daily? Once you've identified these, you can associate them with it and use them as opportunities to pause and connect. Self-check-ins create space and serve as a reset. They also allow you to attend to a need or concept and set a boundary. The practice helps you in breaking free from an *all-or-nothing mentality*. You will not only develop self-awareness, but you will also gain confidence, reduce stress, and increase your resilience.

Here are some questions you can ask yourself during a self-check in:

- What am I feeling right now?
- What thoughts are going through my head?
- What do I need right now?
- What can I do to take care of myself?
- What is my intention for the next task or transition?
- What are my boundaries and how can I enforce them?
- How can I stay present and focused?

It is important to be non-judgmental and accepting of your answers, even if they are not ideal or comfortable. The goal of self-check-ins is to gain awareness and understanding of yourself, not to criticize or punish yourself. Here are some times you can practice self-check-ins:

- When you wake up
- Before a meeting or important task
- During a break
- When you feel stressed or overwhelmed
- Before bed

Regularly practicing self-check-ins can help you to stay grounded, focused and present. It can also help you to manage stress, process emotions, and make better decisions.

Body acceptance

What would you say if asked to explain your relationship with your body? Is it based on mutual respect and cooperation, or is it a tug-of-war between two foes seeking ultimate dominance? Would you say that you adore your body? We live in a world that teaches us to detach from our bodies and, at worst, to despise them. We are trained from a young age to distrust our bodies, strive to control them, and compel them to submit. We blame ourselves when our stubborn bodies refuse to submit. In this climate, appreciating our bodies can be a risky proposition. However, appreciating our body can seem like an unattainable goal.

Many people find embracing their bodies to be overwhelming and like a demand placed on them. While no one is required to love their body, some of the dislikes of the term stem from misunderstandings about what it means to love your body. When we say *"love your body,"* we usually mean that we must love how it looks. But that is not quite right. If we focus on how we look, we continue to support a system that teaches us that our appearance is the most important aspect of ourselves. Positive body image is knowing that your body is good, not *believing* it is good, regardless of how it looks. If you only love your body when you like how you look, that is not love. That is *objectification*. When we say *"love your body,"* we should mean that we love it fiercely and unconditionally, as you would love a child, pet, or valued friend or family member. This is a love that does not rely on your body constantly doing what you want it to do or looking the way you want it to. It is the kind of love that can withstand a fight or even betrayal. Love exists even when we do not like our bodies. And it is this love that enables us to be sympathetic toward our bodies, even when they are failing us.

As spring arrives and we shed our protective layers of winter jackets and bulky sweaters, we revisit a wardrobe that may not accommodate the changes our bodies have gone through in the past year. Body image struggles may resurface as we slowly emerge from a year spent mainly in social isolation. The task is not to push these feelings away or pretend they don't exist but to offer ourselves love and compassion during these difficulties.

Did you know that specific behaviors can indicate whether an individual is satisfied or dissatisfied with their body? People with a negative body image are generally unhappy with how they look. They may feel the need to change their body size or shape. Here are some behaviors that may indicate a negative body image:

- Checking appearance in the mirror frequently: People may frequently look in the mirror to see if their body has changed. They may also try to hide their body from view by wearing baggy clothes or avoiding mirrors altogether.
- Measuring body parts: People may measure their body parts to see if they have changed. They may also compare their body measurements to those of others.
- Pinching skin: People may pinch their skin to see if it is loose or saggy. They may also compare their skin to that of others.
- Spending a lot of time on makeup: People may spend a lot of time on makeup to try to cover up their perceived flaws.

They may also avoid going out without makeup, even if they are just running errands.

- Talking a lot about thinness, muscles, or physique: People may frequently talk about thinness, muscles, or physique. They may also make negative comments about their own or others' bodies.

- Consistent negative talk about others' or own appearance: People may frequently make negative comments about their own or others' appearance. They may also focus on the perceived flaws in others' bodies and use these flaws to make themselves feel better about their own body.

- Obsessing over food, weight, calories, dieting, or exercise: People may become obsessed with food, weight, calories, dieting, or exercise. They may spend a lot of time thinking about these things and may feel like they cannot control their thoughts about them.

- Linking food with feelings of shame, guilt, or disgust: People may associate food with negative emotions such as shame, guilt, or disgust. They may feel like they should not eat certain foods or that they should eat very little food.

- Not wanting to leave the house because of the way one looks: People may not want to leave the house because of the way they look. They may feel self-conscious and worry about what others will think of their body.

It is important to remember that not everyone who engages in these behaviors has a negative body image. However, if you are concerned about your body image, it is important to talk to a trusted adult or mental health professional. While it is perfectly normal to become conscious of our bodies and want to look our best, some warning signs can indicate a deeper problem that a mental health professional must address.

Turning negative thoughts around

It is important to be mindful of the thoughts that run through your head when you see yourself in the mirror. Do you speak kindly to your body? Or do you criticize your body for every flaw? Learning to recognize and reframe negative attitudes about your body takes time. However, you may break the mental habit of criticizing your body and learn to think more positive, more accepting thoughts over time. To get started, consider the following options.

1.

Initial thought: *"I look terrible."*

Replacement thought: *"I'm not happy with how I look today, and that's okay. Everyone experiences this at times. However, how I feel about my appearance does not determine my worth."*

It's normal to have days when you don't feel great about your appearance. But it's important to remember that your worth is not determined by how you look. You are much more than your appearance. You are kind, intelligent, funny, and talented. Focus on these qualities instead of dwelling on your perceived flaws.

2.

Initial thought: *"I'll never be beautiful."*

Replacement thought: *"Beauty is subjective. There is no one definition of beauty. I am beautiful in my own way, and I am confident in who I am."*

Beauty is in the eye of the beholder. What one person finds beautiful, another person may not. It's important to remember that beauty is not just about physical appearance. It's also about inner beauty, such as kindness, compassion, and intelligence. When you focus on your inner beauty, you will start to see yourself in a more positive light.

3.

Initial thought: *"I hate my stretch marks."*

Replacement thought: *"My stretch marks are a sign of my strength and resilience. They remind me of all the things I've been through and all the things I've accomplished."*

Stretch marks are a normal part of life. They can happen to anyone, regardless of their weight or size. They are a sign of your body's ability to stretch and grow. Instead of hating your stretch marks, try to see them as a badge of honor.

4.

Initial thought: *"I'm so ugly."*

Replacement thought: *"I am beautiful, inside and out. I am kind, compassionate, and intelligent. I have so much to offer the world."*

Your worth is not determined by your appearance. You are much more than your physical body. You are a complex and multifaceted individual with a wealth of inner beauty. Focus on the things that make you unique and special, and you will start to see yourself in a more positive light.

Body-positive people recognize that the world has many different shapes, sizes, and colors of bodies. They believe that all bodies are deserving of love and respect, regardless of their appearance. They don't believe they have to look a certain way to be happy with themselves. We often feel better when we write about our personal life experiences because it allows us to express ourselves freely. It can also help us to identify and change limiting beliefs that we may have about ourselves.

Writing about your body image can be a powerful way to heal your relationship with your body. It can help you to express your feelings, identify your limiting beliefs, and find support from others. Here are some questions to consider:

1. When have you denied yourself because you felt you hadn't had the *perfect* body? Think about activities you may not have done, an outfit you may not have purchased, a date you may not have gone on.

    _____

    _____

    _____

    _____

    _____

2. Write down three ways your life would change if you started accepting all aspects of who you are without judgment or shame.

    _____

    _____

    _____

    _____

    _____

3. How does social media impact the way you feel about your body? Consider scrolling through any social media app for a few minutes and then answering this question. If it negatively affects, what can you do about that?

_____

_____

_____

_____

_____

4.   How do you define beauty, and what does it mean for you?

_____

_____

_____

_____

_____

5.   What are some things you love about your body today?

_____

_____

_____

_____

_____

Barriers that block you from self-love

If we don't have what we want right now, we may be preventing it in some way. When we're not where we want to be emotionally and mentally, we can feel overwhelmed. Most of us can relate to these obstacles, but focus on the one or two that most resonate with you the most right now.

Perfectionism

Perfectionism is an obstacle to achieving our goals because nothing is perfect. When we set unrealistic expectations for ourselves, we are setting ourselves up for failure. Perfectionism obscures our worth and value, diminishing the benefits and magnifying the flaws. It is an ego trap that blocks us from loving, accepting, and appreciating ourselves. We will never be perfect, and striving for perfectionism can lead to feelings of inadequacy, frustration, and discouragement. It can prevent us from taking risks and trying new things. We may be afraid of making mistakes, so we avoid taking action altogether.

Judgment

When you judge yourself, you are tying yourself to your flaws, inadequacies, and weaknesses. This can lead to low self-esteem, which can make it difficult to heal, transform, and experience your loving inner nature. Instead of judging yourself, try to be compassionate and understanding. Allow yourself to be excused for your mistakes and shortcomings. Remember that everyone makes mistakes and that you are not alone. When you accept yourself for who you are, you are free to grow and evolve. You are also more likely to experience the goodness, truth, and beauty of who you are.

Guilt

Guilt is a painful emotion that can be caused by making a mistake, hurting someone, or not living up to our own expectations. It can keep us stuck in the past and prevent us from moving on. When we feel guilty, we may try to punish ourselves in order to make up for our mistake. This can take many forms, such as self-criticism, self-isolation, or even physical self-harm. However, punishing ourselves does not actually make us feel better. In fact, it can make us feel worse and more trapped in our guilt. The best way to deal with guilt is to accept it and learn from it. This means acknowledging that we made a mistake, but also forgiving ourselves and moving on.

Repressed emotions

When we ignore, reject, or suppress our emotions, we are not honoring or loving ourselves. We are also preventing our hearts from feeling the emotions that they need to feel. Emotions that are buried do not die. In fact, when we suppress or bury painful emotions, we also suppress lighter, good emotions like love, joy, and happiness. We must learn to appreciate our dark and light emotions equally. This means allowing ourselves to feel all of our emotions, without judgment. It also means expressing our emotions in healthy ways. When we do this, we are able to live more fully and authentically.

Comparison

When we compare ourselves to others, we set ourselves up for two outcomes: either we feel superior or inferior. This is a game that we all play far too frequently, and it can be very damaging to our self-esteem. With the advent of social media, comparison has become second nature to most of us. We are constantly bombarded with images and posts of people who seem to be more successful, more beautiful, and happier than we are. This can lead to feelings of inadequacy and low self-esteem. Comparison arises from a lack of self-esteem and an ability to see our own strengths. When we compare ourselves to others, we are essentially saying that we are not good enough. We are settling ourselves up for failure because we are never going to be perfect. The best way to deal with comparison is to focus on ourselves and our own journey. We need to learn to appreciate our own unique qualities and strengths. We also need to remember that everyone is on their own path, and we should not compare ourselves to others.

Feelings of unworthiness

A lack of self-esteem can stem from the belief that you do not deserve anything, including your desires, a particular way of life, admiration, achievement, and everything else that the world has to offer. You may believe that there is something about you that prevents you from getting what you want, but this is not true. Starting a self-love journey involves exploring self-worth, which is not an easy task. However, once you begin to see yourself with greater clarity" life will surprise you with the things you have always wanted.

From self-criticism to inner peace

"I'm so stupid. I'm a failure. I need help to do anything right. Everyone must think I'm an idiot."

These thoughts are often linked to a general sense of not being good enough. They can cause feelings of inadequacy, unworthiness, failure, and shame. They can be about one's abilities, intelligence, physical attractiveness, thoughts or emotions. Our predisposition to self-criticism often stems from our early childhood interactions. For example, our parents may have had unrealistic expectations for us. Or we may have had a sibling who excelled academically, athletically, or in other areas and was constantly praised for their performance. Teachers who are overly demanding or punitive coaches may have also contributed to our self-critical tendencies. Our religion or culture may also instill high expectations of ourselves, adding to our sense of not being good enough. This form of an inner critic can also be fueled through friendships. For example, during our adolescence, we may have experienced connections with peers or a boyfriend or girlfriend that further eroded our sense of self. These early experiences may have contributed to excessive perfectionism motivated by a desire to escape shame in the eyes of others.

How to respond to your self-criticism

It is important to remember that we are not our thoughts. Just because we have a self-critical thought does not mean it is true. We can learn to challenge these thoughts and replace them with more positive ones. Here are a few tips for challenging self-critical thoughts:

1. Identify your strengths

Self-critical thoughts can be tough to overcome, but it's important to remember that you are not your thoughts. You are a valuable and worthy person, and you have many strengths. Identifying and reminding yourself of your strengths can help you regain confidence and overcome self-criticism. Here are a few tips for identifying your strengths:

- Think about what you are good at. What are your skills and talents? What do you enjoy doing?
- Ask for feedback from others. What do your friends, family, and colleagues say are your strengths?
- Reflect on your past accomplishments. What have you achieved in your life? What challenges have you overcome?

Once you have identified your strengths, make a list of them and keep it somewhere you can see it often. When you are feeling down, take a look at your list and remind yourself of all the things you are good at. This can help you to challenge negative self-talk and boost your self-confidence. Remember, everyone has strengths and weaknesses. It's important to focus on your strengths and to be kind to yourself about your weaknesses. You are a valuable and worthy person, and you deserve to be happy and confident.

2.   Search for proof

Self-critical thoughts can be very damaging, but it's important to remember that they are often not based on reality. When you have a self-critical thought, ask yourself if you have any factual evidence to back it up. For example, if you think "I did horribly on my exam," ask yourself if you really did. Did you make some mistakes? Sure. But did you also get some things right? Did you study hard? Did you do your best? If the answer is yes to these questions, then you probably didn't do as horribly as you think you did. Everyone makes mistakes. Even the smartest and most talented people make mistakes sometimes. A bad grade on an exam doesn't mean that we're stupid or that we'll never succeed. If we can challenge our self-critical thoughts and replace them with more realistic and positive thoughts, we can start to improve our self-esteem and feel better about ourselves.

3.   Replace self-critical thoughts

When you realize you do not have facts to back up your self-critical thought, consider replacing it with a more realistic one that focuses on improvement rather than criticism. For example, if you think "I am not as successful as I should be," you could replace that thought with "I'm on my own journey and I'm making progress. I'm learning and growing, and I'm getting closer to my goals every day." Everyone has their own definition of success. What is important is that you are working towards your own goals and that you are making progress. Don't compare yourself to others, and don't be afraid to celebrate your own successes, no matter how small they may seem.

4.   Practice self-compassion

When you have a self-critical thought, consider how you would react if a friend conveyed this negative thought to you. Would you speak to them in the same manner? We often forget to be kind to ourselves and to practice self-compassion. It may be helpful to shift your inner dialogue from the first to the third person, as if you were replying to a friend. For example, if you think "I'm going to make a fool of myself. Everyone is going to think I'm an idiot," you could try saying to yourself "I'm feeling really anxious about this presentation, but that's okay. Everyone gets nervous sometimes. I'm going to take some deep breaths and focus on what I know. I'm going to do my best and that's all I can ask for." This type of self-talk can help you to challenge your negative self-image and focus on your strengths and positive qualities. It can also help you to feel more compassion for yourself and to be more understanding of your mistakes.

8

Farewell, yesterday: Soar beyond the past

Reviving our hearts by moving on

Have you ever clung to something you knew was toxic or harmful, and asked yourself, "Why is it so difficult to let go of someone who is wrong for me?" Letting go is a common challenge that everyone experiences at some point in their lives. We have all been in heartbreaking situations where people have wronged us, or things haven't gone as planned. It can be difficult to move on from these experiences. There are many reasons why it can be difficult to let go of something or someone that is wrong for us. Here are a few:

- Fear of the unknown: When we're in a familiar situation, even if it's a bad one, we know what to expect. We know how to cope with the pain and the hurt. But when we let go and move on, we're stepping into the unknown. We don't know what's going to happen next. And that can be scary.
- Attachment: We may be attached to the person or thing we're holding onto, even if it's not good for us. We may have created a bond with them, or we may have invested a lot of time and energy into the relationship. And it can be hard to let go of something we're attached to.

- Hope: We may still be holding onto hope that things will change. We may hope that the person will change their behavior, or that the situation will improve. And as long as we have hope, it can be difficult to let go.
- Guilt: We may feel guilty about letting go. We may feel like we're abandoning the person or thing we're attached to. Or we may feel like we're not good enough to deserve something better. And guilt can keep us stuck in unhealthy relationships or situations.

Letting go is a common piece of advice that we receive from our friends. It sounds simple, but it is often difficult to do. We may be unable to let go of a grudge or a betrayal. The brain reacts differently to negative and positive information. When we experience something negative, our brains tend to focus on it and ruminate on it. This is because our brains are wired to pay attention to threats and danger. So, when we have a negative experience, our brains are constantly scanning for signs that it might happen again. This can make it difficult to let go of the past, because our brains are constantly reminding us of it.

Negative events are processed more deeply by our brains, which makes them easier to recall. This can make it difficult to let go of the past and move on. We may feel like we're stuck on a hamster wheel, reliving painful experiences over and over again. While we cannot change how our brains function, we can train ourselves to get off the hamster wheel. This requires us to release our emotional attachment to the past, especially the negative ones. It can be difficult to accept that someone has wronged us, or to admit that we made a mistake. But doing so is essential for moving on. There is a fine line between honoring the past and becoming consumed by it. We can use our negative experiences as an opportunity to grow, but we cannot let them define us. We must learn to let go of the past and focus on the present moment.

How to stop ruminating

Everyone experiences pain and hurt in their lives. It's natural to want to avoid these feelings, but doing so can prevent us from healing and moving on. Instead of trying to forget the past, we can learn to accept it and let it go.

- Acknowledge your pain. It's important to acknowledge the pain you're feeling, rather than trying to suppress it. This will help you to start to process it and move on.
- Don't blame yourself or others. It's easy to get caught up in blaming ourselves or others for the pain we've experienced. But this doesn't help us to heal. Instead, focus on learning from the past and moving forward.
- Focus on the present moment. It's easy to get caught up in the past, but it's important to focus on the present moment. This will help you to appreciate the good things in your life and to let go of the pain of the past.
- Forgive yourself and others. Forgiveness is essential for letting go of the past. It doesn't mean that you have to forget what happened, but it does mean that you let go of the anger and resentment you may be holding onto.
- Create new memories. One of the best ways to let go of the past is to create new memories. This will help you to focus on the present moment and build a new future for yourself.

Emotional detachment

Life exposes us to a variety of people, things, pleasurable experiences, and challenges. These situations often evoke strong emotions and bring us tears of joy or pain. While this may seem natural, living in this way can make us emotionally weak over time. An emotionally strong person participates in the drama of life without becoming emotionally attached to it. This means being able to create an emotion that is different from the scene in which we are placed. For example, if we are in a crisis situation, we can remain calm and collected even though we may be feeling scared or anxious. This is because our natural state of mind is one of peace and tranquility. On the other hand, an emotionally attached person will be easily overwhelmed by their emotions. If someone behaves rudely, they will become angry or hurt. They may even take the rude behavior personally. This is because they are too attached to their emotions and cannot see the situation objectively. We cannot be stable if our emotions fluctuate a lot. We can shift our focus by accepting that we have been emotionally drained and need stability. If someone has behaved rudely, an attached person will easily get hurt, while the detached person will empathize and forgive. We cannot be stable when our emotions fluctuate a lot. We can shift our focus by accepting that we have been emotionally drained and need stability. One way to do this is to create a positive affirmation and repeat it three times in the morning.

I am a powerful, calm and peaceful person. I am stable, and my feelings are not easily swayed. I am not affected by the way people behave. I give love and respect to all.

This affirmation can help us remember that we are in control of our emotions and that we can choose to be calm and peaceful, regardless of the circumstances.

Attachment and love are often seen as opposites, but they are not. Attachment is the need to possess or control another person, while love is unconditional and unselfish. Attachment can lead to possessiveness, jealousy, and sorrow, while love is uplifting, healing, empowering, and joyful. Attachment is often rooted in insecurity, while love is rooted in security. When we are secure in our identity, we do not need to possess or control others. We can then offer pure love, which is a magnet that attracts people and keeps them together. It is a state of being where we know our identity and do not need to control others. Pure love allows us to move forward and grow. Detachment is not the same as indifference. It is not about not caring for others. It is about caring for them in a way that does not require us to control them. Detachment is about loving others unconditionally and allowing them to be free. When we detach, we can experience pure love. It is the greatest gift we can give ourselves and others.

Endings don't have to be messy

Sometimes, love is not enough to keep a relationship going. People outgrow each other and need to go their separate ways. This is not a failure, but a natural part of life. When we love someone, we help them grow and evolve. We teach them things, and they teach us something. We share our experiences and our hearts with each other, and in the process, we both become better people. If we are lucky, our love will last a lifetime. But even if it doesn't, it doesn't mean that our love was a failure. It simply means that it was time for us to move on. When we walk away from a relationship, we believe there is something better for us. We believe that there is someone who will love us and cherish us in the way that we deserve to be loved and cherished. It takes bravery to walk away from a relationship, even if it is the right thing to do. It takes courage to believe in ourselves and to believe that we deserve to be happy. So, if you ever decide to leave a relationship, remember that it is not a failure. It is simply a sign that you are ready for something more.

Being alone doesn't mean being lonely. It can be a time for healing, transformation, and self-discovery. When you are alone, you have the time and space to focus on yourself. You can figure out what you like and don't like, what you want out of life, and who you are. You can try out different activities and learn new things. Being alone can be empowering. It gives you the freedom to choose and live on your own terms. You don't have to compromise with anyone else. You can do what you want, when you want, and how you want. If you feel lonely, try to focus on the positive aspects of being alone. Use this time to get to know yourself better and build a strong foundation for your future.

Letting go of someone you care deeply about can be one of the most difficult things you will ever do. You may have done everything you could to make the relationship work, but sometimes, it's just not enough. This is because love is not always enough. Sometimes, two people are meant to be separate. Sometimes, their love changes. And sometimes, life gets in the way. It's important to remember that none of this is a reflection of your worth. You are worthy of love, no matter what. And it is not your fault if someone cannot give you the love you deserve. It's okay to let go. It's okay to move on. And finding someone who will love you for who you are is okay.

Breakups can be hurtful, but they can also be a learning experience. They can help you to understand what you want and need in a relationship. They can also help you identify things you don't want in a relationship. When you are going through a breakup, it is important to allow yourself to feel your emotions. It is also important to take some time to heal and figure out what you want next. Once you have had time to heal, it is crucial to start thinking about what you want in a relationship. What are your deal breakers? What are your must-haves? Once you know what you want, you can look for someone who meets your needs. Remember that you are worthy of love and respect. Don't settle for anything less than what you deserve.

We all have wounds in our past. We have all been hurt by people we love, experienced loss, and faced challenges we thought we would never overcome. But we do overcome. We heal, we grow, we become stronger. We may not forget the pain we have experienced, but we can learn from it. We can use it to make us better people. We can use it to build resilience. We can also use it to help others.

We can share our stories with others who are struggling. We can offer them hope and support. We are all survivors. We have all been through hard things, but we have all come out the other side. We are stronger than we think we are. We are capable of more than we know. So, don't give up. Keep fighting, keep healing, and keep growing.

Your thoughts create your reality

Our thoughts and beliefs create our reality. We cannot control everything that happens to us, but we can control how we react. Negative thoughts lead to negative emotions and harmful behaviors, while positive thoughts lead to positive emotions and positive behaviors. Our thoughts and beliefs also shape our reality in other ways. For example, if we believe in ourselves, we are more likely to take action and persevere in facing challenges. On the other hand, if we believe that we cannot achieve our goals, we are less likely to succeed. It is important to remember that we can change our thoughts and beliefs. We can do this by challenging negative thoughts, focusing on the positive, and practicing gratitude. When we change our views and opinions, we change our reality. We can create an enriching life by thinking positively and believing in ourselves.

Many people feel offended by the notion that we create our own reality. They see it as a form of victim blaming. After all, no one asks for bad things to happen to them. However, it is helpful to understand that life is made up of three components: *things we control, things we influence, and things we have no control over.*

Things we control: These are the things that we have direct control over. For example, we can control our thoughts, our actions, and our emotions.

Things we influence: These are the things that we can have some influence over, but not complete control. For example, we can influence our relationships, our careers, and our health.

Things we have no control over: These are the things that we have no control over, such as the weather, other people's actions, and natural disasters.

There are many things in life that we cannot control, such as our families, natural disasters, diseases, job layoffs, the death of loved ones, fires, and car accidents. However, we do have control over how we perceive and interpret the events in our lives, which in turn affects how we feel and behave. For example, if we are in a relationship and our partner leaves us, we could think, "I will never find anyone else to love me again." This thought will likely lead to negative emotions like sadness, disappointment, and hurt. We may also withdraw from social situations and avoid putting ourselves out there again. On the other hand, we could choose to think, "I'm glad this happened. I am saved from being in a meaningless relationship." This thought will likely lead to positive emotions like relief, excitement, and hope. We may also be more open to meeting new people and starting new relationships. The point is that we get to choose what thoughts we think. When we think about something repeatedly, it becomes a belief. Beliefs act as a lens through which we see the world, and they can either limit us or empower us. For example, if we believe that we are not attractive enough, we will likely focus on the negative feedback we receive. We may also interpret neutral or even positive feedback in a negative way. This can lead to us feeling bad about ourselves and avoiding social situations. On the other hand, if we believe that we are attractive, we will be more likely to notice and appreciate the positive feedback we receive. We may also interpret neutral or even negative feedback in a positive way. This can lead to us feeling good about ourselves and being more confident in social situations. Ultimately, we create our own reality by the thoughts we think and the beliefs we hold. If we want to create a positive reality, we need to be mindful of our thoughts and beliefs and challenge any negative ones. We also need to take action in line with our desired reality. For example, if we want to be more confident, we need to put ourselves in situations where we can practice being confident. It is not always easy to change our thoughts and beliefs, but it is possible. With awareness and effort, we can create the reality we want to live in.

While there will always be things that happen outside of our control, we can control how we think and feel about them. The way we think and feel about these events will determine how we react to them and shape our lives. There are always people who thrive in times of crisis. These people are not necessarily lucky. They are more likely to be people who choose to see opportunity amid adversity. It can be difficult to break out of autopilot and take charge of our lives. The more complicated our lives have been, the harder it may seem at first. However, it is possible, and it is worth trying. Henry Ford once said that *whether you think you can or can't, you are right.* Our thoughts have a powerful direct effect on our reality. We are more likely to succeed if we believe we can achieve our goals. On the other hand, if we believe that we cannot achieve our goals, we are less likely to succeed. We can choose to think positively and to believe in ourselves. Doing so makes us more likely to create a positive and fulfilling life.

The difference between letting go and moving on

It happens. You said you would start loving yourself, but a part of you knew you were lying. A part of you has been dying since you parted ways, and you never looked at it again. Years later, it is rotting, and the smell is starting to distract you. A part of you has been fading into an abyss since they left, and you didn't bother getting it back. You just stared at it like an astronaut losing a button of their suit in space. Some of you were left in the same place where they walked away. You realized this as you looked into a complete stranger's face and saw them. There was a resemblance, you admit. But even though you knew they were a different person, you missed them.

As a hopeless romantic, you realize that the art of moving on and letting go is entirely different. You have let go of the person, but you haven't moved on. Memories are traps that keep you from making new ones. Letting go meant that you accepted what happened, but deep down, you were not content. You had to do it because you had no choice but to live your life. Moving on, on the other hand, means that you have gained power. It means that your wounds have healed, even though they haven't completely disappeared. Letting go may have given you peace, but not moving on only held you back. Years have passed, but you are still here where they left you. They say you must move on when it becomes your only option. But because you didn't, you just learned to live a double life: a life that no longer loves them on the outside and another life that craves their presence on the inside.

Now that you admit all this, you only wish for more feelings. You wish for feelings for yourself so huge that they finally remind you of the wreckage inside and the need for your hands to repair these broken pieces. Or, you wish for feelings for someone else to whom you can shower all the love trapped amidst the darkness. You wish for either of these feelings to bloom so beautifully that you again believe in love's goodness. It is scary, but you need it now more than ever. Because one way or another, you have to face and accept that you must grow. You have to look at more strangers' faces and be strong enough not to miss them, or better yet, be healed enough not to be reminded of them. You must move on because only then can you think of them and not feel longing, love, or hope.

Why we can't move on

Forgiveness is often easier said than done. We may tell our friends or loved ones to *forgive and forget*, but it can be a different story when it comes time for us to forgive. There are many reasons why forgiveness can be so challenging. Sometimes, we may feel like we have been wronged so profoundly that we can never forgive the person who hurt us. Other times, we may be afraid that if we forgive the person, they will hurt us again. And still, we may not know how to forgive at different times. If you struggle to forgive someone, it is essential to be patient with yourself. There is no right or wrong timeline for forgiveness. Some people may be able to forgive quickly, while others may need more time.

Forgiving is not about condoning a person's actions. It is simply about letting go of the anger and resentment that you may be feeling. If you are struggling to forgive alone, many resources are available to help you. You can talk to a therapist, counselor, or religious leader. Many books and websites can offer guidance and support. Many people struggle with forgiveness, but with time and effort, you can learn to let go of the pain and move on. Here are some reasons why you may be finding it difficult to detach and move on:

You are not being honest with yourself about the real cause of the hurt

Sometimes, we can convince ourselves that we are angry at someone for one reason when we are actually angry about something else entirely. For instance, we might be angry with our sibling for not attending our party, when in reality, we are secretly furious that they insinuated our marriage won't last. The first reason is easier to be angry about, but if we want to forgive our sibling, we must admit to ourselves what we are really angry about.

You have attached your current wounds to older, deeper wounds

When hurt by someone, it can sometimes trigger older, deeper pains from our past. This can make it difficult to forgive the person who hurt us because we are dealing with the current and all the old pain that has been brought up. This is called the *snowball effect*. Loading new hurt on top of old hurt can become overwhelming and difficult to forgive. For example, if our partner leaves us, we may feel rejected. This feeling of rejection can trigger old feelings of abandonment from our childhood. If we don't deal with these old feelings, we may start to believe that our partner left us because we are not worthy of love. However, our partner may have left us for several reasons that have nothing to do with us. They may have been unhappy in the relationship or have met someone else.

Therapy can help manage the snowball effect. A therapist can help you understand your old pain and how it is affecting your current relationships. They can also help you to develop coping mechanisms for dealing with the pain and to forgive the person who hurt you.

Forgiveness is not about condoning the other person's actions. It is simply about letting go of the anger and resentment that you may be feeling. Forgiveness does not mean that you have to forget what happened or that you have to have a relationship with the person who hurt you. It simply means that you are choosing to let go of the pain and move on with your life.

You mistake forgiving with accepting what they did

Forgiveness is a complex process that involves finding compassion for the other person and their choices, while allowing yourself to heal from the pain they caused you. It does not mean you condone their actions, but rather that you let go of your anger and resentment towards them.

You are scared that forgiving will make you vulnerable

Anger can make us feel tough and like we're protecting ourselves from further hurt. However, anger and resentment can make us more vulnerable in the long run. This is because when we're angry, we're constantly replaying the painful situation. This can erode our sense of worth and make us feel like we are not good enough. Think about the last time you were furious with someone. How did you feel when you saw them? In all likelihood, you felt threatened and very shaken. But then think about how you felt years later when all was forgiven and you had let go of your resentment. Did they then have any power over you at all? The answer is probably no. When we forgive someone, we're not saying what they did was okay. We're saying that we will no longer let their actions control our lives. We choose to let go of the anger and resentment and move on. Forgiveness is not easy, but it's worth it. When we forgive, we free ourselves from anger and resentment. We also open ourselves up to the possibility of healing and growth.

You are getting comfortable with the benefits of having a grievance

Not forgiving someone can make us feel sorry for ourselves and lead us to seek attention from others. This attention can be like a drug we crave more of, as it makes us feel better and wanted. However, forgiveness requires us to let go of our victim mentality and realize that we are ready for the better benefits of moving on. This means being prepared to feel empowered and choose good things for ourselves.

You think that to forgive someone, you have to talk to them

When we forgive someone, we are not doing it for them. We are doing it for ourselves. Forgiveness is about letting go of the anger, resentment, and bitterness that we may be feeling toward the person who hurt us. It is about no longer allowing their actions to control our lives. The other person does not have to know that we have forgiven them. In fact, if we want forgiveness to involve a confrontation, we may not be ready to forgive at all. We may be looking for more drama.

You may be scared of the emotions that can arise if you try to forgive

Forgiveness is a process that can be similar to grieving. It is full of ups and downs and can take time to heal. However, suppressing sadness and anger can have long-term negative effects. It is crucial to allow yourself to feel your emotions and start letting go of the anger and resentment you may be feeling.

You are scared that they won't forgive you back

Forgiveness is not always a two-way street. Sometimes, when we forgive someone, they may not reciprocate. This can be frustrating, but it is essential to remember that forgiveness is about us, not them. When we forgive someone, we do not say what they did was okay. We say we will no longer let their actions control our lives. We are choosing to let go and move on. If we forgive someone *for their sake,* it is not really forgiveness. It is a form of control that puts us in a place of superiority rather than the place of compassion true forgiveness requires. True forgiveness is about letting go of our need to control the other person and their actions. It is about accepting what happened and that we cannot change that. It is about choosing to focus on the present and the future.

You are not ready to forgive

Forgiveness is a process, and it can be challenging. In an ideal world, we could forgive someone simply by deciding to do so. However, the heart has its own timing. If you are not ready to forgive someone, that is okay. You do not have to forgive anyone if you don't want to. The most important thing is to focus on healing and moving forward. This may mean talking to a therapist or talking to a friend. It may also mean doing things that make you happy and help you to relax. Forgiveness is a journey, not a destination.

Releasing thoughts that hold us back

Here is a little exercise to assess the disadvantages of holding onto difficult and distressing thoughts. Think about the questions below and respond as honestly as possible to support your personal development.

1. What is a negative thought that keeps coming back, no matter how hard you try to ignore it?

   _____

   _____

   _____

   _____

   _____

2. What are the emotional and physical symptoms you experience when you get caught up in this negative thought?

   _____

   _____

   _____

   _____

   _____

3. How does your behavior change when you get caught up in this thought?

_____

_____

_____

_____

_____

4. What are the advantages and disadvantages of getting caught up in this thought?

_____

_____

_____

_____

_____

5. How does this distract you from your goals and moral values?

_____

_____

_____

_____

_____

6. What can be a positive way of responding to this thought?

_____

_____

_____

_____

_____

7. To ultimately let go of this thought, what uncomfortable feelings
    will you face?

_____

_____

_____

_____

_____

8. If you choose to do this, how will this help you to live a more
    fulfilling, content, and happy life?

_____

_____

_____

_____

_____

Coping with an unfair world

Life can be unjust and unfair. We may wonder why some people
have more money, are more attractive, or get away with more than
others. Injustice can be hard to swallow, and it can be easy to get
caught up in a cycle of anger, frustration, helplessness, despair, and
revenge. When we see injustice, it can trigger a range of painful
emotions. We may feel angry, frustrated, helpless, despairing,

or even vengeful. The desire for justice is what drives us to seek revenge. We may think that it's not fair that someone should get away with something, and we may want them to suffer the consequences of their actions. However, revenge fantasies don't make the pain go away. They actually keep it alive, feeding the anger and maintaining the helplessness. They can also add shame and guilt to the mix. And of course, carrying out revenge would only make the situation worse. Instead of dwelling on injustice and seeking revenge, we can try to focus on the positive. We can appreciate the good things in our lives, and we can work to make the world a more just place. We can also find ways to cope with our anger and frustration in healthy ways, such as exercise, journaling, or talking to a therapist. It's important to remember that we can't control the actions of others, but we can control our own reactions. We can choose to respond to injustice with compassion and understanding, rather than anger and hatred. We can also choose to take action to make the world a more just place, even if it's just in small ways.

Everyone experiences injustice, but some people suffer more than others. One reason for this is that people who have been frequently victimized have witnessed more intense and blatant episodes of unfairness in their lives. For example, they may have been bullied, discriminated against, or impoverished. However, not everyone in a similar situation experiences the same level of distress about injustice. Additionally, people who have experienced even slight injustice can be just as sensitive. One thing that people who are sensitive to unfairness have in common is *me vs them mentality*. This can quickly lead to anger, strained relationships, and isolation. It's as if you're constantly at odds with an intangible other person or group. So, what should you do if you're someone whose emotions have been painfully stirred by an experience with injustice? Here are some questions to consider:

- What are you feeling?

- What is your perspective on humanity?
- Is your anger a cry for action or a cry of helplessness?
- Are you the sole victim of injustice while everyone else is treated fairly?

If you repeatedly encounter this circle of injustice, it's time to shift your focus away from what is happening in the world and toward what is happening within you.

The truth is that life is unjust. The world is filled with unfairness. We see it every day in the news. We know this truth even as children. We've been coping with it since the first time we saw another child get an ice cream cone and we didn't, or when we were punished for something that we didn't do. We may also be coping with existential unfairness, the aspects of life that we find hardest to accept. For example, that we will all die someday, and that there are no guarantees. Regardless of what we cannot control, we are ultimately responsible for our own lives. It can be helpful to remind ourselves that people do many beautiful things to make the world a better place. There are many people who are constantly seeking to make a difference. If a particular injustice inspires you to act, you could be one of those people, doing your best to help those in need. However, focusing on helping yourself to become a happier, more peaceful, and accepting person will have a far greater positive impact on your life and the people around you than spending your life angry and nursing a grudge. Peace begins with you.

Ho'oponopono Technique to release the past

Ho'oponopono is an ancient Hawaiian practice for forgiveness and reconciliation. This practice is based on the belief that we are all connected and that our thoughts and actions affect others. When we forgive someone, we are also forgiving ourselves. The practice involves four aspects:

Recognition: We recognize that we are all connected and that our thoughts affect others. We acknowledge that our thoughts and actions have the potential to harm others, even if we didn't intend to.

Remorse: We express remorse for any harm we have caused, directly or indirectly. We take responsibility for our actions and our words, and we apologize for the pain we have caused.

Request for forgiveness: We ask for forgiveness from the person we have harmed and the universe. We acknowledge that we need to be forgiven in order to heal, and open ourselves to receiving forgiveness.

Giving thanks: We give thanks for the opportunity to forgive and be forgiven. We recognize that forgiveness is a gift, and we appreciate the chance to let go of anger and resentment.

Ho'oponopono is a powerful practice that can help us to heal from the pain of past hurts and to create a more peaceful and harmonious world. It is a practice that can be used for personal healing, as well as for healing relationships. There are four aspects at work in this prayer: repentance, forgiveness, gratitude, and love. These are embedded in the four phrases that make up the prayer:

"I am sorry; please forgive me. Thank you, I love you."

- I am sorry: This phrase expresses remorse for any harm we have caused, directly or indirectly. It is important to be sincere when we say this phrase, and to take responsibility for our actions.
- Please forgive me. This phrase asks for forgiveness from the person we have harmed and the universe. It is important to be open to receiving forgiveness, and to believe that we are worthy of being forgiven.

- Thank you. This phrase expresses gratitude for the opportunity to forgive and be forgiven. It is important to be grateful for the chance to let go of anger and resentment, and to create a more peaceful world.

- I love you. This phrase expresses love for ourselves, the person we have harmed, and the universe. It is important to remember that we are all connected, and that we are all worthy of love.

It is natural to resist this prayer at first, especially if you have a lot of healing to do. However, if you persevere, you can experience the power of forgiveness and healing. It will help you acknowledge your wrongdoings and take responsibility for them. It will help you let go of the anger and resentment you feel towards the person who has wronged you. You will be able to appreciate the good things in your life, even amid the pain. You can also open your heart to the possibility of healing and transformation.

What's more, you can open your heart to the possibility of healing and transformation. If you are interested in this prayer, you can repeat the phrases silently or aloud. You can repeat them in any order and say them as often as needed. It is also helpful to pay attention to the feelings as you say the words.

When you practice Ho'oponopono, you may find yourself asking questions like:

1. What am I sorry for? This question can help you to identify the ways in which you have harmed yourself or others, either intentionally or unintentionally.

2. Where do I still need forgiveness? This question can help you to identify the areas in your life where you are holding onto anger, resentment, or bitterness.

3. Where do I need to be forgiven? This question can help you to identify the people you have harmed, either intentionally or unintentionally.

4. What am I thankful for? This question can help you to focus on the positive aspects of your life, even in the midst of pain and suffering.

5. Do I really feel loved? This question can help you to assess your own sense of self-worth and value.

6. Why am I worthy of love? This question can help you to challenge any negative beliefs you may have about yourself.

7. Where do I want to feel more love? This question can help you to challenge any negative beliefs you may have about yourself.

The questions that you ask yourself during Ho'oponopono can be just as enlightening as the answers. It is important to let the questions ferment with time. You don't need answers right away. Let them come without forcing them. The healing, reconciliation, and release will take time to sink into your cells and seep through life. Be patient with yourself and with the process.

Here are some additional tips for practicing Ho'oponopono:

- Be patient. This is a process of healing and transformation, and it takes time. Be patient with yourself and with the journey.

- Be gentle with yourself. This is not about beating yourself up or making yourself feel worse. It is about accepting yourself and your flaws, and about letting go of the past.

- Be present. When you are practicing Ho'oponopono, it is important to be present in the moment. Don't dwell on the past or worry about the future. Focus on the present moment and on the healing that is happening.

- Be open to forgiveness. Forgiveness is essential for healing. Be open to forgiving yourself and others, even if it is difficult.

- Be grateful. Gratitude can help to open your heart and to create a more positive outlook on life. Be grateful for the good things in your life, even in the midst of pain and suffering.

9

To love and be loved

What makes relationships tick?

You might be surprised to know that the word *love* appears approximately 2,146 times in Shakespeare's collected works, along with almost 59 instances of the word *beloved* and some 133 uses of the word *loving*. So, what does Shakespeare have to say about the subject?

What is love?

Shakespeare very passionately describes love as:

"Love is not love
Which alters when it alteration finds,
Or bends with the remover to remove:
O no! It is an ever-fixed mark
That looks on tempests and is never shaken."

He meditates on the most authentic and strongest kind of love: the love between minds. He defines such a union as immutable and eternal. Love is one of the most profound emotions known to man. It can take many forms, but for many people, the most fulfilling expression of love is found in a romantic relationship with a compatible partner. For these people, romantic relationships are among the most meaningful aspects of life and a source of deep satisfaction.

The foundation of all relationships

The ability to form healthy, loving relationships is learned. While the need for human connection seems inherent, some research suggests that the ability to develop stable relationships is formed in infancy, in the child's first experiences with a primary caregiver who reliably meets their food needs, nurturing, warmth, protection, and social contact. These relationships are not fated but are thought to establish deeply rooted patterns of relating to others. However, the end of such a relationship is often a source of great psychological turmoil.

Attachment styles

Why are some people distant and disconnected in their relationships, while others are clingy and need constant reassurance? It is because different people have different attachment styles. A person's attachment style is formed and developed in early childhood in response to their relationships with their first attachment figures, such as their parents or caregivers. Our attachment style as adults is believed to mirror our dynamics with our caregivers as infants and children. Attachment style encompasses how we respond emotionally to others, how we usually interact with relationship partners, and how we generally behave in relationships.

Secure attachment style

Secure attachment style refers to forming secure, loving relationships with others. People with a secure attachment style can trust and be trusted by others, love and accept love, and quickly get close to others. They are not afraid of intimacy and do not panic when their partners need time or distance from them. They can rely on others without becoming totally dependent. Secure attachment is considered the healthy ideal for all relationships.

Anxious attachment style

Anxious attachment style is characterized by an intense fear of abandonment. People with anxious attachment style tend to be very uncertain in their relationships. They often worry that their partner might leave them, so they always seek reassurance. Anxious attachment style is associated with *neediness* or *clingy* behavior in relationships, such as becoming very worried if your partner does not text you back quickly enough and constantly feeling like your partner doesn't care enough about you.

Avoidant attachment style

Avoidant attachment style is characterized by a fear of intimacy. People with avoidant attachment style typically have difficulty getting close to others or trusting others in a relationship. They may find it difficult to express their emotions, and they may withdraw from relationships when they feel overwhelmed. They may even find their relationships stifling and avoid them altogether because they prefer to be independent and rely on themselves.

Disorganized attachment style

Disorganized attachment style is a combination of the anxious and avoidant attachment styles. People with this attachment style desperately crave affection, but at the same time, want to avoid it at costs. They are reluctant to form close romantic relationships but at the same time, have an urgent need to feel loved by others. The attachment behavior of these individuals can appear inconsistent and fluctuate between the extremes of avoidance and anxiety. It is associated with psychological and emotional risks, including difficulty regulating emotions, increased sexual behavior, and increased risk for violence in their relationships.

To conclude, let's take a closer look at the signs of each of these attachment styles in the given comparison table:

Secure Attachment	Anxious Attachment	Avoidant Attachment	Disorganized Attachment
Is comfortable with open discussions	Does not have clear boundaries	Avoids emotional intimacy	Has an extreme need for closeness coupled with the tendency to avoid it
Empathizes well	Has poor emotional regulation	Is conflict-avoiding	Shows aggressive behavior
Respects boundaries	Needs constant reassurance	Strongly fears rejection	Has negative self-image
Is comfortable with commitment	Becomes overly fixated on others	Rarely asks for help from others	Has deep-rooted shame
Is honest and straightforward	Craves intimacy but can't trust easily	Has high anxiety	Feels inadequate or unlovable
Not afraid to share feelings	Is afraid of being alone	Has low self-esteem	Has low self-worth
Disagrees without losing calm	Avoids connecting with others	Accuses partner of being clingy	Has depression and/or anxiety

How we find love

Finding a partner to share your life with can be a hopeful, complicated, and challenging task. Finding a suitable partner is considered one of the most important tasks of adulthood. People spend enormous amounts of thought and energy on the task, whether flirting at a coffee shop, scouring hundreds of online profiles, or asking friends or relatives to arrange dates. However, you may have to go far outside your comfort zone to find someone you feel comfortable with for the rest of your life.

The laws of attraction

There are some universal factors that make us attracted to others, at least momentarily. For example, men are attracted to women who are physically young and healthy because they appear to be the most fertile. However, you don't have to be exceptionally attractive to find a mate. You just need to be attractive enough to seduce your partner. People who mate tend to have similar levels of attractiveness. We seek out people who are similar to us, with some exceptions. Did you know that people judge whether a potential mate is attractive in a fraction of a second? Men are more likely than women to find their potential partners attractive and are more likely to base their judgments on appearance. What about love at first sight? People believe they experience love at first sight, but that's probably a false memory. This phenomenon is rarely mutual and isn't real love because it usually doesn't involve intimacy, commitment, or passion. Human attraction is a complex and fascinating phenomenon. In most cases, it involves people who are similar or familiar than different. Some identical twins have even married each other, and many have even married the widow of a sibling. However, when opposites attract, such as partners of different ages or sizes, they can thrive, even if others condemn those against the grain.

Finding The One

Even people who date frequently and are open to meeting new people may need help finding long-term love. The most successful couples meet through shared social networks or while pursuing a common interest. Couples with weaker social ties take longer to enter into marriage. Novelty can also be a deciding factor in relationship success. A partner who challenges you to grow and learn may be a lifelong companion. Finding the right partner may start with physical attraction, but it is the personality that usually keeps couples together. People who are emotionally stable and likable are more likely to have satisfying long-term relationships. In the exciting early stages of a relationship, we tend to ignore unpleasant traits. However, these traits may become more pronounced over time, which can lead to conflict and ultimately the end of the relationship.

Therefore, we should take our time with a long-term commitment and postpone possible conflicts. People who believe there is one perfect person for them, a soulmate, may have difficulty finding love. When people believe that their partner must be perfect, they are more likely to end relationships that have a real chance of succeeding than to discuss conflicts that might be resolvable. Those who believe love is a journey and that relationships undoubtedly have ups and downs are much more likely to be satisfied. There is a reason why some people end up in the same failed relationships repeatedly. They are frequently attracted to the same type of partner, often because of sexual attraction. It is not so easy to fall in love with someone who looks great, but you do not immediately find attractive. However, when people are willing to devote time to someone who might be a good fit for them, they often find that they can actually develop an attraction towards them over time. Friends can also become lovers, but that can happen only under certain circumstances. Partners who differ in attractiveness tend to have known each other long before becoming a couple. In other words, they started out as friends.

How we commit

The decision to marry or commit in a less formal but equally emotionally significant way is a big step for many couples. While it is impossible to truly know another person, a romantic commitment can be made with greater confidence and hope when partners feel equally devoted to each other and express this through their words and behavior. Knowing whether feelings for a partner are mutual can be challenging, but research points to some relatively sure signs that a relationship is developing. These signs include frequently initiating conversations and responding quickly, using more *we* than *I* in discussions, a lack of hesitation when it comes to spending time together, and consistent, simple gestures of affection such as holding hands, hugging, and sitting or being close.

Love is hard to define, but many people believe it includes passion, intimacy, and commitment. These three aspects are known as *consummate love.* To find out if you are in love, ask yourself questions such as:

1. How often do I think about this person?
2. How well do they know me?
3. Do I feel responsible for them?
4. Am I all in with them?

In the early stages of a relationship, couples who are more socially engaged are usually the most satisfied. However, why do some people resist commitment? People are more likely to commit when they can rely on a partner and are generally satisfied with how their partner meets their needs. On the other hand, people who resist commitment may have multiple relationship alternatives, such as friends with benefits. Other obligations that take up their time and attention can also prevent partners from giving their relationship the attention it deserves.

Maintaining a relationship

Strong relationships require different types of care, such as physical, emotional, and attentive care. Certain qualities are essential in maintaining healthy relationships. For instance, everyone should have confidence that their partner will give them time and attention. Both partners must also be willing to deal with and face the inevitable differences and challenges.

The benefits of togetherness

In the most successful relationships, partners give each other the benefit of doubt and take active steps to foster a strong sense of belonging. In the long run, this connection gives people a solid emotional foundation to pursue their dreams and bounce back quickly when setbacks occur. In healthy relationships, our partners see us more positively than anyone else, perhaps more thoroughly than we see ourselves. We can use their belief in us to move closer to our ideal selves. This is called the *Michelangelo Effect* because just as the great sculptor could look at a slab of stone and see an ideal, hidden human form, our partner's positive messages and signals of support can help us evolve. A healthy relationship should move towards personal growth and help you strive to become your best. With the committed support of a partner, people recover better from stress or trauma, appreciate life more, and are more open to learning. Experienced partners know they can't make each other the people they most want to be with, but they can help each other achieve their personal goals. By enabling the other person to take the first step, reminding them of their strengths, and helping them identify damaging habits, a partner can help the person they love to grow and find greater personal satisfaction. It is rare to find a partner who is perfect in every way or meets all of the items on the list of qualities one hopes to find in a spouse. An important factor in relationship success is understanding that this role model doesn't exist and setting aside the checklist once you have settled on your partner. It may feel like a compromise, but a good enough relationship is often more than good in the long run.

Striving for intimacy

Although *intimacy* is often used as a euphemism for sex, it is not exclusively a physical connection and is not limited solely to romantic relationships. Intimacy involves the risk of exposure. It usually begins cautiously in conversation, sharing something emotionally significant with a new partner, but grows over time into a connection with someone we believe genuinely understands us. Once a bond of intimacy is forged, it can become the basis of deep friendship and physical desire. Feeling emotionally safe, relaxed, and open can be essential for true intimacy. When one partner gives in to criticism or contempt and attacks the other, it can undermine intimacy by triggering the other's self-defense mechanisms and undermining their trust. This is one of the reasons why couples need many more positive interactions with each other than negative ones to maintain a healthy relationship. Sustaining a relationship requires some basic measures of respect, which include attention, affection, honesty, and gratitude from one's partner, as well as a willingness to address conflicts and share the household workload. A prolonged lack of these can jeopardize the future of a relationship, which is why partners must address these issues when they become a problem. More than 80% of people in committed relationships say their partner is their best friend. Being part of such a *two-in-one* relationship or experiencing *companionate love* has significant emotional benefits, starting with the likelihood of a long-term relationship. A person cannot feel secure in a relationship if their partner criticizes them too much or constantly tries to correct their perceived weaknesses. In the long run, it is easy to get frustrated with your partner's habits and criticize when they refuse to change, but taking a step back and seeing a flaw in the context of the entire relationship should help you find the perspective and acceptance you need to sustain your relationship.

Challenges in relationships

The success or failure of relationships in adulthood has many causes that are not solely determined by the partners' childhood experiences. Most people need to acquire the skills necessary to sustain romantic relationships and make them flourish, and threats to their relationships can be a major source of psychological anxiety.

Resilience in relationships

For centuries, couples did not typically spend several decades together as they do today due to shorter life expectancy and higher medical risk. So, the challenges facing long-term partners today can be seen as novel. However, fundamentally, relationships are challenged because people change, and their partners are forced to adapt. However, many couples face the same crossroads when crises threaten their relationships, such as the first year together, the birth of children, their eventual departure, the decline of old age, and the inevitable tragedies everyone experiences. A couple's relationship can deteriorate if they are constantly exposed to polarizing experiences such as jealousy, goal-blocking, closed communication, avoiding complex topics, and taking conflict personally. Recognizing these potential crises early and talking about them openly can save a relationship. So, how do the most successful couples handle challenges? The most critical factor determining whether a couple can survive challenges in their relationship is whether they believe they can. Partners who are confident that they will stay together, no matter what conflicts arise, and who believe they have the skills to sustain their relationship are much more likely to stay together long-term. Even in couples where both partners work outside the home, it is common for one of them to earn much more than the other or enjoy more success or prestige in society. When they met, the partner often did not seem to be on that path. However, envy can be avoided if partners honestly acknowledge and appreciate each other's strengths and try to support each other wherever they are.

Long distance couples often find that they feel the same intimacy, communication, commitment, and sexual satisfaction as other couples. In fact, some studies have shown that couples with the most significant geographic distance are even happier than those who live only a short distance apart. People who successfully manage a long-distance relationship tend to be less stressed, more positive, and more confident in their ability to sustain a relationship.

Facing infidelity

Being faithful to a spouse or partner is important to many people. However, infidelity does happen, and it can pose a severe challenge to the offending partner and the relationship. Whether a couple survives infidelity depends on a number of factors, such as the stability of the relationship, the nature of the affair, and the support of the couple's social network. Discovering that a partner has cheated can be upsetting and even traumatic. However, it does not always mean the end of the relationship. Many couples find a way to stay together and rebuilt trust. The decision of whether to stay or leave is a personal one, and there is no right or wrong answer. The social network of the cheated partner can play a significant role in their decision. If the partner's friends and family are supportive of the relationship, they may be more likely to stay together. However, if the friends and family are critical of the relationship, they may be more likely to encourage the partner to leave. Ultimately, the decision of whether to stay or leave is up to the individual couple. There is no right or wrong answer, and what works for one couple may not work for another.

People cheat in relationships for a variety of reasons. The most common reasons are disappointment, seeking variety, feeling neglected, taking advantage of a tempting opportunity, boosting self-esteem, anger, lack of commitment, and strong sexual desire. Jealousy is a painful and undesirable emotion that can cause anger, insecurity, self-doubt, and embarrassment. It is also almost universal in relationships. One teaching is to listen to jealousy and not make it taboo because it can indicate an imbalance in the relationship or a real threat from someone outside the relationship. It can also be an aphrodisiac, reminding us how passionately we feel about a partner.

When partners are different

Many couples of different ages, sizes, cultural backgrounds, ethnicities, or religions can be happy together. In surveys, they tend to say the same thing: the challenges they face are real but primarily external and not internal. The ability to block out the judgment of others, whether strangers or close relatives, is critical to their long-term satisfaction. Historically, women generally indicate that they prefer a slightly older man and men a slightly younger woman. However, there are also many couples with a much more significant age difference, with the man usually being the older partner. A key to their success is *perceived age* – women think their more senior partner is younger than others, and older partners also think of themselves as more youthful than their biological age. Couples in which the woman is the much older partner are less common but no less successful. Often the woman has a stronger sex drive than other partners her age and is looking for a younger partner who can keep up with her, try new things, and let her take control of herself. Some younger men want to court older women because they value their attention and experience. They may also find greater equality in the relationship.

The end of relationships

Some people can leave behind years of marriage and immediately feel relieved and unburdened. For others, the end of a relationship that lasted only a few weeks can cause intense emotional trauma that lingers for years. Regardless of the circumstances surrounding a breakup, it can be a significant stressor in life. The effects on one's ego and self-esteem should not be ignored.

Why do couples split?

In some failed relationships, partners experience a gradual decline in connectedness, intimacy, and affection. In contrast, in others, one or the other partner may recognize the moment they knew it was over. When a relationship becomes strained, couples must decide whether they have built a relationship that can sustain them and, if not, whether it is best to end it. Many sources of conflict include affection, communication, jealousy, sexual frequency, control, future plans, housework and responsibilities, secrets, and finances. By being aware of these issues that frustrate couples, new partners can better prepare themselves and stay together longer. Psychologist John Gottman is known to have identified four core issues that are most likely to derail a relationship:

1. Criticism: This is when one partner constantly points out the other's flaws.
2. Contempt: This is when one partner shows disrespect or disdain for the other.
3. Defensiveness: This is when one partner refuses to take responsibility for their actions or words.

4. Stonewalling: This is when one partner withdraws from communication and refuses to engage with the other.

When negative interactions outweigh positive ones, a couple may not survive. Sometimes, the signs that a relationship has become toxic can only be recognized after the fact. This is because if a partner is suffering from gaslighting, intermittent positive reinforcement, social isolation, or a sense that they can't be themselves in their primary relationship, it often takes a while for them to recognize this or admit to themselves that they need to leave the relationship. The most common reasons people give for falling out of love are:

- Loss of physical intimacy
- Loss of trust
- Loss of feeling loved
- Emotional pain, often triggered by grief over feeling lonely
- Negative self-perception (poor self-image and feeling rejected by their partner)

A husband's negative feelings toward his wife's friends are a fairly reliable predictor of divorce. This may be because women are more likely to share their relationship problems with friends, or because the wife's friendships are closer than the husband's and therefore seen as a threat to the relationship. The termination of a relationship may occur at different stages, such as:

- Reflection: Beginning to think about a change
- Preparation: Preparing to end the relationship
- Action: Initiating the separation
- Maintenance: Sticking with the decision

Ghosting is an increasingly common way to end a relationship. It happens when a partner suddenly cuts off all contact and disappears without explanation. Ghosting can be very hurtful because it leaves the abandoned partner feeling confused, rejected, and unworthy of love. There are many reasons why people ghost their partners. Some people do it because they are afraid of confrontation, while others do it because they don't want to deal with the emotional fallout of a breakup. Whatever the reason, ghosting is never a good way to end a relationship. If you are thinking about ghosting your partner, please reconsider. There are much better ways to end a relationship, such as:

- Having a conversation: This may be difficult, but it is the most respectful way to end a relationship. Sit down with your partner and explain why you are breaking up. Be honest and direct, but also kind.
- Writing a letter: If you can't face your partner in person, you can write them a letter explaining why you are breaking up. This can be a good option if you are feeling too emotional to have a conversation.
- Seeing a therapist: If you are struggling to end the relationship on your own, you can see a therapist for help. A therapist can help you to communicate your feelings to your partner in a healthy way and to come to a mutually agreed-upon end to the relationship.

Getting over a breakup

Even if you didn't think a relationship would last a lifetime, its end can be painful, especially if you feel you've been rejected by someone you loved and trusted. Understanding why breakups are painful and what you can learn from them are essential steps to getting back on your feet. Here are some ways to get over a breakup:

- Keep your distance from your ex. This can be difficult, but it's important to give yourself time and space to heal.

- Take up new activities. This is a great way to meet new people and distract yourself from your ex.
- Maintain your health. Eating healthy, getting enough sleep, and exercising can help you to feel better both physically and emotionally.
- Repeat positive mantras. Some people find that repeating positive phrases or mantras can help them to stay positive and focused on the future.

Here are some challenges that people face after a breakup:

- Catastrophizing: People who tend to catastrophize may have a harder time seeing a positive future after a breakup. They may dwell on negative thoughts and what-ifs, making it difficult to move on.
- Low self-esteem: People with low self-esteem may wonder who they are without their partner. They may also have difficulty entering into a new relationship.
- Adopting poor health habits: Men are more likely to adopt poor health habits after a breakup than women. This may be because they are more likely to depend on their partner as their primary source of emotional support.
- Turning to close friendships for help: Women are more likely to turn to close friendships for help after a breakup than men. This may be because they have a stronger support network of friends and family.

Here are some tips for breaking up with someone:

- Make an appointment to talk. This will give you both time to prepare for the conversation and to be respectful of each other's feelings.
- Speak honestly but not critically. It's important to be honest

about why you're breaking up, but it's also important to avoid being critical of your partner.
- Say what you value about the other person. Even though you're breaking up, it's important to acknowledge the good times you had together and to express your appreciation for the other person.
- Set clear boundaries. Once you've broken up, it's important to set clear boundaries about contact and communication. This will help you to move on and to heal.

When love is one-sided

Unrequited love is when you have strong romantic feelings for someone who does not share those feelings. It is a one-sided relationship that can be painful and embarrassing. It can be difficult to tell if love is unrequited, and it can cause a great deal of uncertainty and emotional distress. Unrequited love can manifest in different ways, including:

- Loving someone who does not return your feelings
- Desiring someone who is unavailable
- The mutual attraction between two people who are in different relationships
- The desire for a former partner after a relationship has ended

The reason why someone might experience unrequited love can vary. Sometimes, it is because the other person is simply not interested in us that way. Other times, it may be because we have idealized the other person in our minds and don't see them as a real, flawed person. Still other times, it may be because we have insecure attachment style and feel more comfortable in relationships that are unattainable. No matter the reason, unrequited love can be difficult experience to deal with. Some of the potential consequences of unrequited love include:

Poor self-esteem

If you continue to have strong feelings of love for someone who does not reciprocate them, your self-esteem may suffer. You may feel rejected and inadequate, and you may question your worth as a person.

Isolation

You may feel isolated and lonely when someone does not reciprocate your feelings. This is especially true if you do not pursue relationships with others.

Stress

Positive relationships serve as a buffer against the detrimental consequences of stress.

Loving someone who does not reciprocate your feelings can be a difficult and painful experience. It can lead to feelings of sadness, stress, and even depression. However, it is important to remember that you are not alone and that there are things you can do to cope with unrequited love. Here are a few tips for coping with unrequited love:

- Acknowledge your feelings. It is important to acknowledge your feelings and to allow yourself to grieve the loss of the relationship. Bottling up your emotions will only make things worse.
- Talk to someone you trust. Talking to a friend, family member, or therapist can help you to process your feelings and get support.
- Give yourself time to heal. It takes time to get over

unrequited love. Don't expect to feel better overnight. Be patient with yourself and allow yourself to heal at your own pace.

- Focus on yourself. Spend time doing things that make you happy and that make you feel good about yourself. This will help you feel good about yourself. This will help you to move on from the unrequited love and focus on your own happiness.
- Avoid contact with the person you love. This may be difficult, but it is important to give yourself space to heal.
- Set boundaries. If you do interact with the person you love, set clear boundaries about what you are and are not willing to do.
- Focus on the positive aspects of your life. Make a list of all the things you are grateful for, both in your life and in your yourself.
- Take care of yourself. Make sure you are eating healthy, getting enough sleep, and exercising.
- Seek professional help. If you are struggling to cope with unrequited love, please seek professional help. A therapist can help you to understand your feelings and develop healthy coping mechanisms.

Unrequited love can be a painful experience, but it is important to remember that you are not alone. There are people who can help you through this difficult time.

Green lights and red flags

It is important to know what behaviors are *green lights* and *red flags* in relationships. Green lights are positive behaviors that indicate a healthy and supportive relationship. Red flags are negative behaviors that indicate a toxic or abusive relationship.

Here are some examples of green lights:

Green lights

Respect	Healthy relationships are based on feelings of admiration and appreciation. Respect is shown when we speak kindly and truthfully to someone and behave in a way that shows we value their time and opinion.
Trust	Trust is when we believe that someone has good intentions and will act in our best interest, even when we are not around.
Communication	Communication is essential for any healthy relationship. It means being able to share our thoughts and feelings with our partner in a clear and respectful way.
Honesty	Honesty is another essential ingredient for a healthy relationship. It means being truthful with our partner, even when it is difficult.
Patience	Patience is important for any relationship, but it is especially important for healthy relationships. We all make mistakes, and our partners should be able to forgive us and give us the time to learn and grow.
Flexibility	Life is unpredictable, and our relationships need to be able to bend and change with it.
Empathy	Empathy is the ability to understand and share the feelings of another person. It is essential for building strong relationships, as it allows us to connect with our partners on a deeper level.
Reciprocity	Reciprocity is the idea of giving and taking in equal measure. Both partners should feel like they are getting something out of it.
Appreciation	When we appreciate someone, we are showing them that we value them and their contributions to our lives. We can express appreciation in many ways, such as through words of affirmation, acts of service, gifts, or quality time.
Space and safety	People need space to grow and develop as individuals. They also need to feel safe in their relationships, knowing that they can be themselves without judgment. This means being able to express their thoughts and feelings freely, even if they are different from our own.

Questions, risks, feedback, and mistakes	In a successful relationship, it is okay to ask questions, take risks, give honest feedback, and make mistakes. This shows that we are open to learning and growing, and that we trust our partner to support us.
Individuality and boundaries	It is important to be able to be ourselves in a relationship. This means having our own hobbies, interests, goals, and friends. We should also be able to set boundaries with our partner, so that we can have a healthy balance of independence and togetherness.

Red flags

Contempt	Contempt can be hidden through sarcasm, condescension, cruel humor, insults, or making fun of someone. It conveys the idea that one person is superior to the other.
Suspicion	Suspicion stems from not believing that someone is looking out for your best interests. It can manifest as attempts to track someone's whereabouts, regulate their behavior, or limit their relationships with others, even if those relationships are healthy and supportive.
Lack of communication	This can lead to emotional distancing, anger, or changing the subject. It can also include dominating conversations by not allowing others to speak or not listening when they do.
Dishonesty	This can manifest as either willfully stating untruths or withholding information.
Impatience	This is characterized by constant annoyance with the natural ebb and flow of life and unrealistic or unfeasible expectations.
Inflexibility	Rigidity is the expectation that things will always be the same. It is accountability taken to its extreme.
Dependence and conformity	This requires giving up one's autonomy and adhering to rigid relationship rules. It also requires that problems in the relationship be kept private, even from trusted and supportive people.
Lack of reciprocity	This occurs when one person insists on meeting their own needs but is unwilling to consider the needs of others, asks for rules to be bent for them, or rarely contributes to joint efforts.

Lack of empathy	Lack of empathy is demonstrated by a refusal or inability to consider another person's point of view and the reasons for their feelings.
Lack of appreciation	This is demonstrated by overlooking someone's efforts, failing to express gratitude, or failing to appreciate someone's contributions.
Lack of growth	In red-flag relationships, there is little room for growth. If the focus is on minimizing mistakes, there is no opportunity for learning and evolving.
Poor conflict resolution	This can involve yelling or physical harm, misplaced blame, defensiveness, overgeneralization, a desire to win, failing to listen to the other person, making assumptions, etc.

Must-have conversations

A relationship can only survive with a strong foundation built on healthy communication. To ensure that couples are on the same page, here is a list of must-have conversations:

Type of conversation	Aim	Where to approach the topic?
Trust and commitment	Talk about building trust and discussing what commitment means to you	Anywhere that reminds you of the first time you fell in love, such as your home or a location with a view
Conflict management	Discuss your similarities and differences and how you will deal with conflicts when they arise	Anywhere you can speak privately, such as a coffee shop or your living room
Sex and physical intimacy	Discuss sexual boundaries and explore each other's sexual frequency. Talk openly about the past.	A private romantic space, such as a bedroom or a secluded spot in nature

Work and money	Discuss your ideas about spending, saving, and investing. Discuss your future plans.	A place that is wealthy and comfortable, such as a high-end restaurant or a luxury hotel
Family	Discuss the type of family you want to raise and the compromises you can make when differences arise	A park or playground
Fun and adventure	Discuss ways in which you can have fun as a couple. Share adventure stories from the past.	A beach or park
Personal growth	Talk about how the relationship has helped you grow and what you can do to help the other grow.	A peaceful or sacred place, such as a church or a meditation center
Ambitions	Share your dreams and discuss how you can support each other and pursue each other's dreams	Any place that inspires you, such as a museum or a concert hall

10

The silent language of grief

Changing shape, but never ending

Loss is the one thing that binds us all together as human beings. It is a painful and heart-wrenching experience that we will all face at some point in our lives. Whether it is the death of a loved one, the loss of a job, a relationship, or something else, loss is a part of the human experience. Grief is the natural response to loss. It is a process of emotional, physical, and spiritual adjustment to a significant change in one's life. Grief can be difficult and overwhelming, but it is important to allow yourself to feel your emotions and to seek support from others. Loss and grief are so common that they are rarely diagnosed as a disorder.

A story about grief

Before we dive into the topic itself, how about a short story?

Julia and her husband had been happily married for 35 years. At 60, her husband passed away after a long battle with cancer. His cancer was not discovered until it was advanced, and he underwent surgery, hormone therapy, and chemotherapy. Julia stayed by his side every day, hoping for a recovery, but he became weaker with each treatment. He was ill for nearly two years, and was transferred to a hospice three weeks before his death. Julia realized at that point that her husband would never return.

They had been married for 35 years and had three children and six grandchildren. They had seen many good and bad times together, but they always loved each other. Julia's husband had a drinking problem, which was a source of tension in their marriage. However, they were committed to each other and looked forward to spending their retirement together. When Julia's husband was diagnosed with cancer, she became his caregiver. This was difficult for both of them because her husband was very independent. As the cancer progressed, he became weaker and needed more help with daily tasks. Julia found caring for him to be difficult and stressful, but she never complained and tried to hide how it was affecting her. She experienced a range of emotions as he was transferred to hospice.

Julia was terrified and knew that her husband's death was near. She was worried about how she would cope without him, but she also felt relieved that she would no longer have to shoulder the physical burden of caring for him around the clock. This made her feel guilty and ashamed. She visited her husband every day when he was in hospice. She read to him, played his favorite music, and helped the nurses care for him. On the day he died, she left the hospice to buy cakes for the staff. When she returned, she found that he had passed away peacefully. She felt terrible for not being by his side in his final moments, and she kept replaying in her head.

After her husband died, Julia's life and home felt empty. Her relatives were constantly in the house, and she was kept busy with funeral preparations. When things finally settled down, she felt lost and didn't know what to do with herself. She had been so focused on her husband for so long that she couldn't remember life before him. Part of her felt relieved that he was no longer in pain. She had been expecting his death for some time, as he had been ill for a while. However, she was unprepared for the overwhelming grief and longing she felt after he died. She constantly replayed all the things she wished she had not said and done differently, such as not arguing with him about his drinking. She also thought about the future they would never have together. She couldn't imagine her life without him.

Julia tried to keep herself busy to distract herself from her pain. Fortunately, her children and grandchildren lived nearby, so she was able to immerse herself in their lives and help with childcare. Her children praised her for her strength and how she was handling her situation. But inside, she knew how hard she was working to suppress her true feelings. She would feel sick to her stomach when she heard his favorite music on the radio. Keeping herself busy helped her get through the days, but she couldn't sleep at night. She would long for her husband and the life they had envisioned for themselves in retirement. Her lack of sleep exhausted her. Eventually, her grief caught up with her and engulfed her. She couldn't get out of bed in the morning and felt as if all the joy had been sucked out of her life.

Understanding loss

When we talk about loss, we often refer to the death of someone we care about. But it's important to remember that people can experience grief when faced with other losses, such as the end of a relationship, the loss of a job, or the diagnosis of a serious illness.

The death of a loved one is a particularly difficult loss to cope with. It is often accompanied by multiple losses, including:

- The physical loss of the person
- The loss of a shared life
- The loss of a shared future
- The loss of support and companionship that the person provided

The circumstances of the loss can also have an impact on how you grieve. For example, a sudden death can be more difficult to cope with than a death that was expected. The age of the person who died, the nature of the relationship you had with them, and your own personal circumstances can also affect how you grieve.

Here are some features of the loss that can influence how you grieve:

The manner of death and whether you had time to prepare for it

1. Expected/anticipated:

For example, you may have foreseen that a loved one would die after a long illness. Their death was no less impactful, but in these cases, some people report that they began to grieve before the person died or when they learned of the illness.

2. Unexpected:

You may have lost a loved one unexpectedly due to a medical crisis or an accident. It is natural to feel shock and disbelief as your mind and body try to process what has happened.

3. Traumatic/violent:

Your loved one may have experienced a violent death or died by suicide. These situations often involve additional layers of shock and grief.

The nature of the relationship you shared with them

The nature and quality of your relationship with the individual can influence the type and intensity of grief you experience. The degree of emotional connection you had with this person, their role in your life, and your sentiments for them when they were alive are all factors that can influence how you grieve for them.

The reactions of others

The reactions of others can either help or hinder your grief. People around us often want us to feel better, but this can sometimes mean they don't give us the space to express our feelings.

What else is happening in your life

Other factors in your life can also impact how much space you have to grieve. You may feel pressured to care for others, keep up appearances, or return to work sooner than you would prefer.

What is grief?

Grief is more than just sadness. As grief progresses, you may find yourself overwhelmed by a range of emotions and physical sensations. The experience of grief is unique to each individual, and it often comes in waves that can be intense and overwhelming at first. These waves can appear out of nowhere or be triggered by reminders of the person you have lost. When you first lose someone, it can feel like you are continuously being battered by massive waves of grief. These waves can be so close together that you may feel like you can barely catch your breath between them. Over time, the size and intensity of these waves tend to decrease, with longer intervals between them. As the weeks, months, and years pass, you will experience many *firsts* without your loved one. Your first dinner out, shopping trip, and birthday without them will all be occasions when you will feel their absence and experience waves of grief. This is perfectly normal.

The effects of grief can be categorized into thoughts, feelings, and behaviors. However, it is important to remember that everyone experiences grief differently. Some people may experience all of these effects, while others may only experience a few. There is no right or wrong way to grieve.

Thoughts (how you might think and remember)

Thinking that you have been treated unfairly	Thoughts about what you should have said or done	Remembering arguments or conversations	Thinking about how they are in peace now
Worries about how you will cope	Thoughts about how life is going to be different	Happy memories	Dreams or nightmares
Anger at the person for leaving you	Thoughts about what you are going to miss	Seeing or hearing your loved one	Thinking about how their suffering has ended

Emotions and physical effects (how you might feel emotionally and, in your body)

Fear and anxiety	Hopelessness and Helplessness	Irritability	Difficulty sleeping or eating
Guilt	Sadness	Fatigue	Feeling sick
Regret	Yearning and longing	Emptiness	Shock and disbelief
Anger	Frustration	Numbness	Heartache

Behavior (how you might act)

Ruminating and overthinking	Stop doing things you used to	Looking at old photos	Carrying on as normal
Avoiding reminders	Keeping busy	Behaving recklessly	Remembering them

Avoiding being alone	Staying in bed	Drinking alcohol	Taking drugs
Avoid being around people	Going through their belongings	Visiting their resting place	Speaking to people who were close to them

There is no right or wrong way to grieve, and there is no right amount of time to grieve. However, some people's grief may linger longer than others, take a different path, and not seem to improve with time as we would expect. This is sometimes referred to as *Prolonged Grief Disorder (PGD)*. The main difference between *normal grief* and *PGD* is that severe grief reactions in PGD last much longer than expected and profoundly impact the bereaved person's life. If you are experiencing PGD, you may feel as if you are constantly in the grip of loss and are overcome by an immense longing for the person you have lost. It can be difficult to go about your everyday life, and you may find that you cannot perform the activities you used to, such as working, socializing, and seeing friends and family. PGD is more common after a severe loss, such as the death of a child or the death of a loved one in unexpected, violent, or stressful circumstances.

Loss is like a wound

When someone you care about passes away, you may feel wounded by their death. Loss is often described as an open, painful wound that needs to be healed. Like a physical injury, the pain of loss is intense at first. The wound is all you can think about; it consumes you, and any movement reminds you of it. At this early stage, you may be so preoccupied with your injuries that friends and family need to take extra care to look after you and be there for you. Grief is often described as the process of recovering from a wound. Wounds will heal naturally over time if the conditions are right. However, it can be too painful to acknowledge or treat a wound, so time doesn't always heal in the way we would like. If an injury goes untreated, it can become infected, making the pain worse. Just like an infected wound, grief needs to be cared for in order to heal. Talking about what happened and how you feel is a good way to tend to your grief and help it heal. It doesn't remove the injury. After all, a significant injury does leave a scar. However, as time and life pass, it becomes a part of you and no longer hurts as much.

Continuing bonds

Some ways of thinking about grief describe stages that people go through, often ending with acceptance or investing in a new life. It is believed that when a loved one dies, you go through a period of adjustment and redefine your relationship with that person, but your bond with them remains strong.

A relationship never ends, and grieving is not something you go through to let go or move on from your loved one. Instead, mourning is the act of forming a new relationship with them. Although your loved one is no longer physically there, you can learn to remember them, and they can live on in your memories and heart. This will imply different things for different people. For instance, it could mean that you continue to say goodnight to them and tell them about your day, maintain some of the routines and activities you performed together, or go to their favorite destination on their birthday. They are remembered, not forgotten.

Life grows around grief

The idea is that we don't get over the pain. It doesn't go away. Instead, as time passes, we learn to grow despite our loss.

Imagine drawing a circle on a sheet of paper. This circle represents you and your life. Now, shade a piece of that circle to reflect your sadness. It may nearly fill your entire life circle immediately after your loss. Many people believe that as time passes, the darkened area of the circle shrinks as the grief fades. However, the opposite might be true. Instead of the shaded area shrinking, the outside circle expands. You and your life expand around the pain. There will be many *firsts*, new experiences, and ups and downs throughout your life. You may begin to reconnect with your family and friends, meet new people, resume socializing, and perhaps experience moments of joy and happiness. As these events accumulate, the outside circle expands. As this happens, your pain remains, but it no longer dominates, making it more bearable. Your life grows around your grief in this way, and you continue to carry it with you.

The 5 stages of grief

Many mental health experts and researchers have spent years researching loss and its accompanying emotions to better understand the grieving process. Elizabeth Kübler-Ross, a Swiss American psychiatrist, was one of these experts. She developed a model based on the five stages of grief and loss.

Exploring the five stages of grief can help you understand and contextualize where you are in your personal grieving process and how you feel. Similarly, if you are concerned about or trying to understand someone else's grieving process, remember there is no one right way to go through it. Everyone grieves in their own way. You may experience a wide range of overwhelming emotions, or you may appear to react in no way. Both responses are valid. The amount of time spent exploring the stages of grief varies from person to person. Understanding and healing from a loss could take hours, months, or even years. You may not go through all five grief stages in the order listed below. You may move back and forth between the stages. You may even skip some of the feelings and deal with your loss in a different way. The five stages of grief are meant to be a *guideline*, not a rule.

Denial: The First Stage

Denial is a defense mechanism that helps us minimize the enormous pain of loss. As we process the truth of our loss, we also try to survive the emotional agony. It can be difficult to accept that we have to say goodbye to an important person, especially if we had just spoken with them the previous week or the day before. Our reality has completely changed in this stage of grief. It may take time for our minds to adjust to this new reality. We reflect on our experiences with the person we lost, and we may question how we will move forward without this person. This is a lot of information to process. Denial seeks to slow down this process and guide us through it one step at a time, rather than risk being overwhelmed by our emotions.

As an immediate reaction, you might first doubt the loss's reality. Consider the following examples:

1.   If you are facing the loss of a loved one, you might fantasize that someone would call to say that there was a mistake and nothing happened.
2.   If you are going through a breakup, you might convince yourself that your lover will soon regret leaving and come back to you.
3.   If you lost your job, you might believe that your former boss will rehire you once they realize they made a mistake.

Denial is a temporary defense mechanism that helps us cope with the initial wave of pain. When we are ready, the emotions we have denied will resurface, and our healing journey will continue.

Anger: The Second Stage

Anger is the second stage of grief. We are trying to adjust to a new world and will likely feel severe emotional distress. There is so much to comprehend that anger may seem to provide an emotional outlet. Remember that being angry does not require us to be vulnerable. It may feel more socially acceptable than admitting we are afraid. Anger allows us to express our emotions without fear of being judged or rejected.

Anger is often the first emotion we experience when we experience our grief. This can make us feel alone in our experience. It can also make us appear unapproachable to others at times when we could benefit from comfort, connection, and reassurance. During the anger stage, you may wonder, "Why me?" or "What did I do to deserve this?" You could also feel a sense of anger towards inanimate objects, strangers, friends, or family members. You might be angry with life. It is not uncommon to feel resentment towards the situation or the person you have lost. Rationally, you know the person is not at fault. Still, you may dislike them emotionally for giving you pain or leaving you. You may even feel guilty for being angry at some point, which can aggravate you. Remind yourself that beneath your anger lies hurt. Anger is important for healing, even if it doesn't feel like it.

Bargaining: The Third Stage

It is common to feel so desperate while coping with loss that you are willing to do everything to lessen or reduce the pain. During this stage of grief, you may try to bargain to change the situation, promising to do anything in exchange for relief from your anguish. When bargaining begins, we frequently direct our desires to a higher power or something larger than ourselves that may be able to influence a different conclusion. During the grieving process, bargaining can take the form of several promises, such as:

1. "God, if you can heal this person, I will turn my life around."
2. "I promise to be better if you let this person live."
3. "I'll never get angry again if you can stop them from dying or leaving me."

Bargaining stems from a sense of powerlessness and gives us a false sense of control over something that seems out of our hands. When we bargain, we try to make deals with a higher power or with fate in the hopes of changing the outcome of a situation. We may focus on our personal flaws or regrets, hoping that by changing our behavior, we can alter the course of events. For example, we may reflect on our relationships with the person we are losing and regret the times we felt distant or caused them pain. We may think about times when we said something we didn't mean and wish we could take it back. We may also assume that if things had gone differently, we wouldn't be in such an emotionally difficult situation. Bargaining is a normal part of the grieving process. It is not a sign of weakness or a lack of faith. It is simply a way for our minds to cope with the pain of loss. If you are experiencing bargaining, it is important to allow yourself to feel this emotion. There is no need to fight it. Just know that it is a temporary defense mechanism that will eventually pass.

Depression

When we are grieving, there comes a point when our imaginations calm down, and we begin to look at the reality of our current circumstances. Bargaining is no longer an option; we must accept what is happening.

We begin to experience the loss of our loved one more intensely at this stage of grief. Our fear begins to fade, the emotional fog lifts, and the loss becomes more tangible and unavoidable. As the sadness intensifies, we tend to withdraw within. We may find ourselves withdrawing, becoming less sociable, and communicating with others less about our problems. Although this is a normal part of the grieving process, living with depression can be difficult. All of this is usually temporary and directly results from the grieving process. As difficult as it may feel at this time, this step is an essential part of your recovery process.

Acceptance

Acceptance does not always mean agreeing with what happened. It is understandable if you never feel this way, depending on your experience. Acceptance is about how you recognize your losses, learn to live with them, and adjust your life accordingly. During this stage, you may feel more comfortable reaching out to friends and family. However, it is also natural to choose to withdraw at times. You may also go back and forth between stages, which is normal. Eventually, you might find yourself stationed at this stage for long periods. This does not mean that you will never feel sad or angry about your loss again. However, your long-term perspective on it and how you deal with it will be different. You will no longer resist the reality of your situation, and you will no longer struggle to make it different.

How can I help myself to grieve?

There are many things you can do to help yourself move through grief. Here are a few suggestions:

Rituals and customs

Rituals help us cope with grief and honor and appreciate our loved ones who have passed away. They are so important that all societies have their own grief rituals. Funerals are ceremonies in which we say our final goodbyes, mourn the loss, or celebrate the departed's life. In cultures where the deceased are cremated, the ashes are often spread at a site of rest. It is also customary for family and friends to pay their respects to the deceased's family and discuss how the person died. From a psychological point of view, these rituals have value and serve two essential functions: They help us make sense of what has happened and address the reality of the loss. They provide a way to express our grief and to connect with others who are also grieving. You can create your own traditions to remember and celebrate your loved one. Some people, for example, opt to plant a tree or host a memorial service in their favorite location. You could consider what would be meaningful for you:

How would you like to commemorate the life of a loved one? What do you want to do to remember your loved one on your anniversary?

_____

_____

_____

_____

_____

_____

Talking about your grief can help you begin to accept your loss. Finding close friends or family members with whom you feel comfortable discussing your feelings can be helpful. Another effective way to express your grief is to keep a journal and write about your feelings. Some people find it beneficial to share their feelings with a therapist. Remember that sometimes other people want to make you feel better. Although this is well-intended, it could also mean that they are trying to cheer you up when you need to talk.

If you want to talk, don't be afraid to let others know that you don't need them to make it better; you need space to be heard.

Make a memory box

Some people believe that it is important to keep a loved one's memory alive after their death. One way to do this is to create a *memory box*. A memory box is a container that holds items that remind you of your loved one. These items could include photos, letters, clothing, jewelry, or anything else that has special meaning to you. Once you have collected your items, you can put them in a box with your loved one's name or a special message. You can then place the box in a special place in your home. You can visit your memory box whenever you feel like it. This could be on your loved one's birthday, anniversary, or any other day that you feel like remembering them. Looking through your memory box can help you to connect with your loved one and to keep their memory alive.

Talking about your story of grief

Talking about your loss and telling the story of your loss and grief can help you to process what has happened. Whether you lost your loved one suddenly or after a long illness, there is often much to process and come to terms with. As your mind tries to make sense of your loss, you may feel a need and even an urgency to tell your story and make sense of what has happened. This can be an essential way of processing all the emotions that you are feeling. If you don't think that you've had a proper chance to speak about what happened, then you might find it helpful to write your story from your perspective, as if you are telling someone about what happened. If you decide to give it a shot, here are some pointers to help you get started:

1. What was happening in your life immediately before you
    learned about your loved one's death? If they were ill, you might
    write about what happened immediately before discovering
    they would die.

    _____

    _____

    _____

    _____

    _____

    _____

2. If your loved one was ill, you might write about when they
    were diagnosed, the medical interventions they underwent,
    and your interactions with the medical professionals. Consider
    how you were affected, your thoughts and feelings, and what
    it was like.

    _____

    _____

    _____

    _____

    _____

    _____

3. Write about the moment you learned a loved one had died. How
    did they perish? What happened? This moment is vivid, and
    people often say they felt shocked. What were you doing at the
    time? How did you feel? What did you do or think? How has

your loss affected you? Reflect on your feelings, thoughts, and grief affecting your life.

_____

_____

_____

_____

_____

_____

Tackling avoidance

In the early stages of grief, doing things that remind you of your loved one may be too difficult. As time passes, it is important to confront the places and events you have been avoiding. Here are some tips:

1. Make a list of everything you have been avoiding. This could include places, activities, people, or tasks. For example, the swimming pool where you used to meet, the restaurant where you used to eat, or certain people who remind you of them.

2. Rank the items on your list from easiest to hardest to confront. This will help you to gradually face your fears and to avoid feeling overwhelmed.

3. Plan how and when you will confront each item on your list. Be kind to yourself and see if you can find a friend or family member to accompany you at first.

4. Pace yourself. You don't have to do everything at once. It may be difficult to reintroduce reminders, so be patient with yourself and take your time.

Write a letter to your loved one

Sometimes our feelings for our loved ones are complicated. While they were alive, either of you may have said or done things that were unpleasant or that you regret. Writing to a loved one can be an excellent way to work through emotions. Try to express yourself and say all you wish you had said.

- There is nothing you cannot say. This is a personal letter, and no one else should see it. Allow yourself to write freely from the heart.
- Tell your loved one what you didn't get to say to them. You could inform them how you are doing since they passed away. You could include the good and the bad.
- Tell them how you remember and honor them. You can share the memories that mean the most to you.
- Express your regrets or your feelings regarding any unresolved difficulties. You can tell them how you feel and may wish to mention different aspects of yourself.

When you are finished, consider what you want to do with your letter. You might either keep it somewhere safe or dispose of it. There is no right or wrong answer, be kind to yourself and do what feels right for you.

Confronting difficult decisions

The death of a loved one can be a very difficult time, and it is not uncommon to feel overwhelmed by the decisions that need to be made. If you lived together, you may need to make financial decisions, move home, or deal with other practical matters. Even the smallest of decisions can feel overwhelming in the early days. It is often advisable to postpone any major decisions until six to twelve months have passed. This will give you time to grieve and to come to terms with your loss. If major decisions are unavoidable, you may need help to think through your options clearly. Consider talking to a trusted friend or family member, or to a grief counselor. A classic problem-solving strategy is to write down what the problem is. Then, brainstorm the options that are available to you: what possible solutions are there? Think of each solution's advantages and disadvantages, and weigh which is the most helpful and wise decision for all concerned. Once you have decided, plan what you need to do to carry out your chosen solution.

These suggestions may make more sense at different stages of your grief journey. For example, talking to someone you trust may be more helpful when your grief is fresh, while journaling may be more helpful when you have had some time to process what has happened. Please don't feel obligated to try all of these suggestions immediately. Some may be more appropriate for you than others. The most important thing is to find what works for you and to give yourself time to heal.

Tasks of grief

William Worden's model of grief uses the acronym TEAR to describe the four tasks of grief. There is no particular order to these tasks, and grieving usually involves going back and forth between tasks as you learn to process your loss.

T = To accept the reality of loss

Accepting the reality of loss means accepting that your loved one has passed away. In the first few days, it is natural to want to deny what has happened, perhaps even wishing to avoid the pain of grief. However, denial can hinder grief and can make you feel worse in the long run. Sometimes, it can be tough to swallow the loss when your loved one dies in tragic circumstances such as an accident or suicide. You may not want to think about how the deceased died, which can prevent you from accepting the reality of their death. Rituals and ceremonies related to someone's death can help you accept that your loved one is physically no more.

E = Experience the pain of loss

This task is about working through the pain of grief. We live in a world where many people have learned to suppress or avoid difficult feelings. Others around you may also want you to be okay, so finding space to process your emotions can be difficult. Avoiding our feelings, however, does not make them go away but can cause grief to continue. The way we feel after a loss is different for everyone. There is no formula for what feelings we need to process. Grief is different for everyone. It is natural to feel sadness, longing, anger, relief, despair, fear, numbness, guilt, shame, or regret. Whatever you feel, it is vital that you find ways to process and deal with your pain however it affects you. This may mean talking about it with people you trust or seeking therapy.

A = Adjusting to a new life

Adjusting to a life without your loved one will take time. You may even feel guilty, but it is important to remember that this is a normal part of the grieving process. The process will be different for everyone. It will depend on your relationship with your loved one, and how much of your life you spent together, and your individual coping mechanisms. For example, if you lose a good friend who was a great support and confidant, you will need to find new ways to connect with others and do things you may have done together. You may need to join a support group, start seeing a therapist, or reach out to other friends and family members for support. If you have lost your life partner, you may need to figure out how to do all the things your partner used to do. You may need to learn new skills, such as how to cook, clean, or do yard work. You may also need to make new friends and find new activities to fill your time. It is important to be patient with yourself during this time. There is no right or wrong way to grieve. Allow yourself to feel your emotions and don't be afraid to ask for help.

R = Reinvest in your new reality.

Reinvesting in the new reality means finding ways to strengthen the emotional connection with your loved ones. This involves living your new life while holding up the memories of your loved one and allowing them to live on in your heart and memories. It means something different for each person. For many, it means engaging in new connections and things that bring joy and meaning back into their lives.

And ultimately, always remember...

While emotions can be all-consuming, they are not permanent. Here are a few thoughts to keep in mind as you navigate through the journey of grief:

It won't feel like this forever

Just ride the wave. Try to find support, take care of yourself, and allow it to go.

You can handle it, even when you feel like you can't

If we try to suppress or avoid our feelings, they can become all the more intense when something triggers them. We can exercise our resilience and build our inner resources by giving painful emotions space.

Be gentle with yourself

Care for your body during times of intense stress can be highly beneficial. Take time to nap, eat nutrient-rich foods, and drink plenty of water. Alcohol and sugar may seem like a quick fix, but they can have just the opposite effect.

Think in cycles, not lines

If you reach a point where you feel good, only to feel bad again, that is not a sign that you have relapsed or are getting worse. That's just how grief works, and it is actually a forward movement. People say, "I was walking down the street, and suddenly, I started crying, and I don't understand because I was feeling so calm." Grief is a series of loops. You can go back to where you were some time ago. It's not impossible.

Your feelings are normal

The pain of grief itself is hard enough to bear. It can be even more complicated when others around you tell you what to do or what not to do. Don't stop yourself from feeling what you feel: anger, sadness, even relief. All feelings that come with grief are valid. Everyone comes to their loss experience with their story, context, and meaning. Whatever you feel at any given moment, it always makes sense. It is valid.

Grief can beget meaning

You cannot *get over* the loss of a loved one. Instead, you can find ways to integrate the loss into your life as you move on. Grief is a natural reaction to loving someone. Although we all have past experiences that can affect our self-image, grief allows us to reflect on what is most important to us. These sources of meaning are a reason to go into life each day, despite the pain you may be experiencing. These touchstones might include a reflection on the person you want to be facing life's challenges. Reflecting on your options for facing suffering can be a powerful exercise.

You're not alone

Yes, you are not alone. You have a community of people who care about you and want to help. This includes your family, friends, and mental health professionals.

Conclusion

Well, folks, we've made it!

You have journeyed through the chapters of this book, learning about the many aspects of mental health and self-improvement. You have explored the dark corners of your mind, and you have come out of it stronger. You have faced your fears, and you have learned to love yourself. You have let go of the past, and you are ready to embrace the future.

So, pat yourself on the back, take a deep breath, and enjoy the amazing feeling of accomplishment. You've done it! You've conquered the jungle and emerged as a champion of mental wellness. This is not the end of your journey, but it is a significant milestone. You have now armed yourself with the knowledge and tools you need to continue on your path to happiness and fulfillment. You are no longer a victim of your emotions, but a master of your mind.

The road ahead may not always be easy, but you are now equipped to handle whatever challenges come your way. You are strong, you are resilient, and you are capable of anything you set your mind to.

So go forth and live your best life! Be kind to yourself, be patient with yourself, and never give up on yourself. You are worthy of happiness, and you deserve to live a fulfilling life.

The journey ahead is yours to take. May you walk it with courage, with hope, and with love.

This book may be over, but remember, you're the author of your life story now.

You've got this, superstar!